The TRUE DEATH of BILLY THE KID

nbm GRAPHIC NOVELS

Nantier • Beall • Minoustchine
NEW YORK

THE
TRUE DEATH
OF
BILLY THE KID

BEING AN
AUTHENTIC NARRATIVE
OF THE
FINAL DAYS
IN HIS
BRIEF AND
TURBULENT LIFE

WRITTEN AND ILLUSTRATED BY
RICK GEARY

Also available by Geary:
A Treasury of Victorian Murder:
Vol. I, pb., E-book
Jack The Ripper, pb., E-book
The Borden Tragedy, pb.
The Fatal Bullet, pb, E-book
The Mystery of Mary Rogers, hc., E-book
The Beast of Chicago, E-book
The Murder of Abraham Lincoln, pb., hc., E-book
The Bloody Benders, pb., E-book
The Case of Madeleine Smith, pb., hc.
A Treasury of Victorian Murder Compendium I, pb.
A Treasury of Victorian Murder Compendium II, hc.
A Treasury of XXth Century Murder:
The Lindbergh Child, pb., hc., E-book
Famous Players, pb., hc., E-book
The Axe-Man of New Orleans, hc., E-book
The Lives of Sacco & Vanzetti, pb., E-book
Lovers Lane, hc., E-book
Madison Square Tragedy, hc., E-book
Black Dahlia, hc., E-book
A Treasury of XXth Century Murder Compendium I, hc.
Fiction:
Louise Brooks, Detective, hc., E-book

see more on these and order at our website:
nbmpub.com

We have over 200 titles
Catalog available upon request
NBM
160 Broadway, Suite 700, East Wing,
New York, NY 10038

ISBN: 978-1-68112-134-5
Library of Congress Control Number: 2017961134
© 2014 Rick Geary
Previously published in a limited run
for a Kickstarter campaign
Printed in China

1st printing March 2018

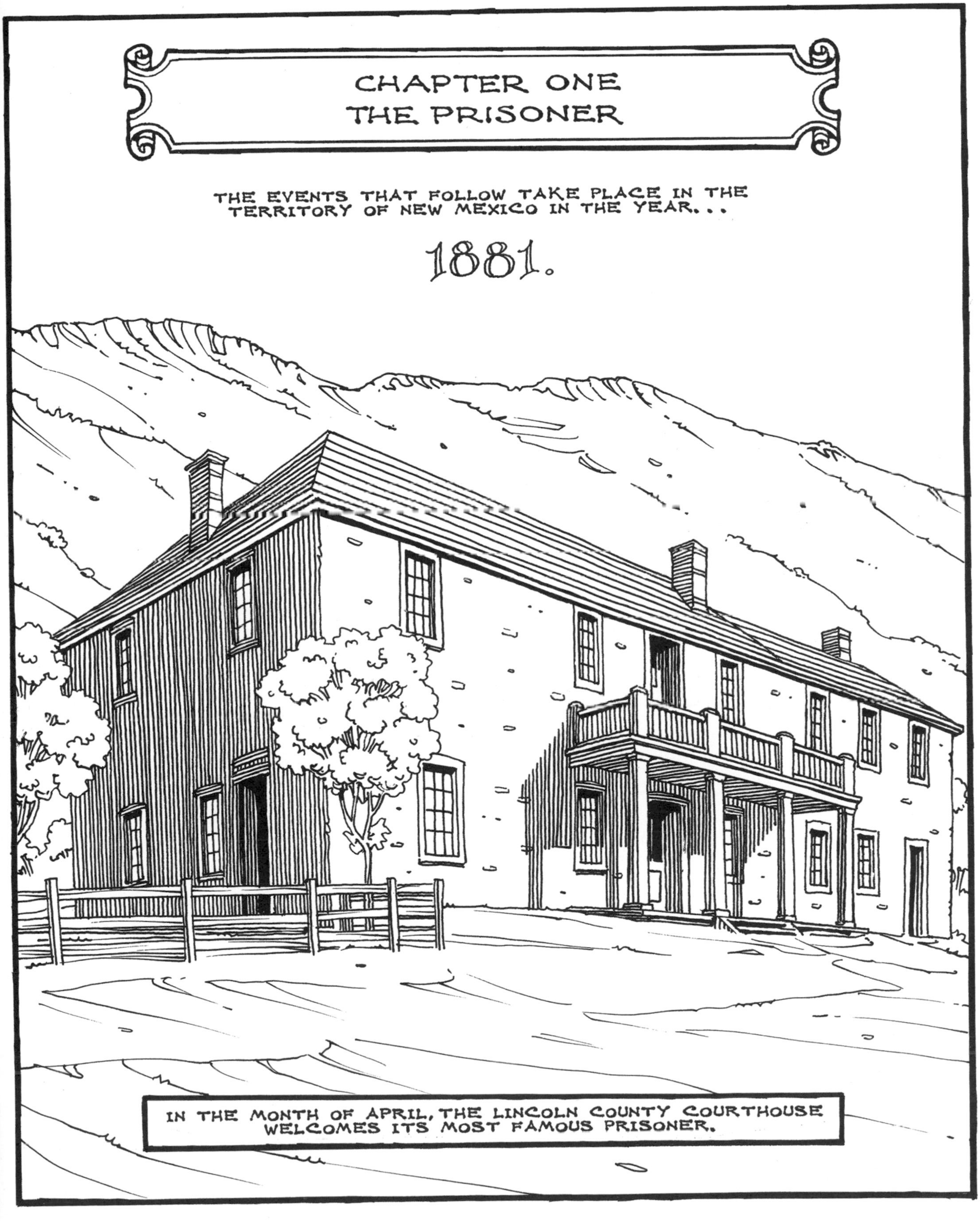
CHAPTER ONE
THE PRISONER
THE EVENTS THAT FOLLOW TAKE PLACE IN THE TERRITORY OF NEW MEXICO IN THE YEAR...
1881.
IN THE MONTH OF APRIL, THE LINCOLN COUNTY COURTHOUSE WELCOMES ITS MOST FAMOUS PRISONER.

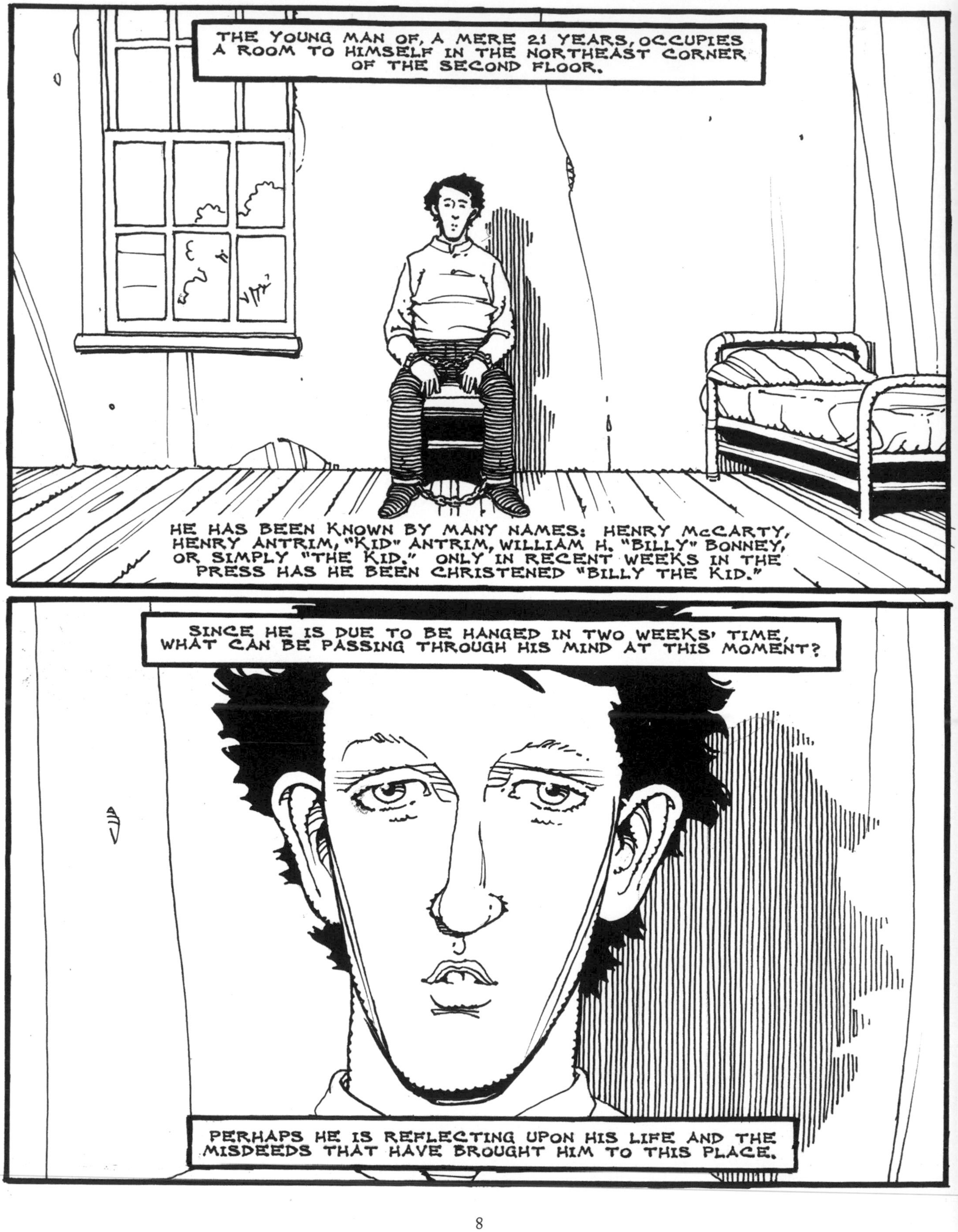
THE YOUNG MAN OF, A MERE 21 YEARS, OCCUPIES A ROOM TO HIMSELF IN THE NORTHEAST CORNER OF THE SECOND FLOOR.
HE HAS BEEN KNOWN BY MANY NAMES: HENRY McCARTY, HENRY ANTRIM, "KID" ANTRIM, WILLIAM H. "BILLY" BONNEY, OR SIMPLY "THE KID." ONLY IN RECENT WEEKS IN THE PRESS HAS HE BEEN CHRISTENED "BILLY THE KID."
SINCE HE IS DUE TO BE HANGED IN TWO WEEKS' TIME, WHAT CAN BE PASSING THROUGH HIS MIND AT THIS MOMENT?
PERHAPS HE IS REFLECTING UPON HIS LIFE AND THE MISDEEDS THAT HAVE BROUGHT HIM TO THIS PLACE.

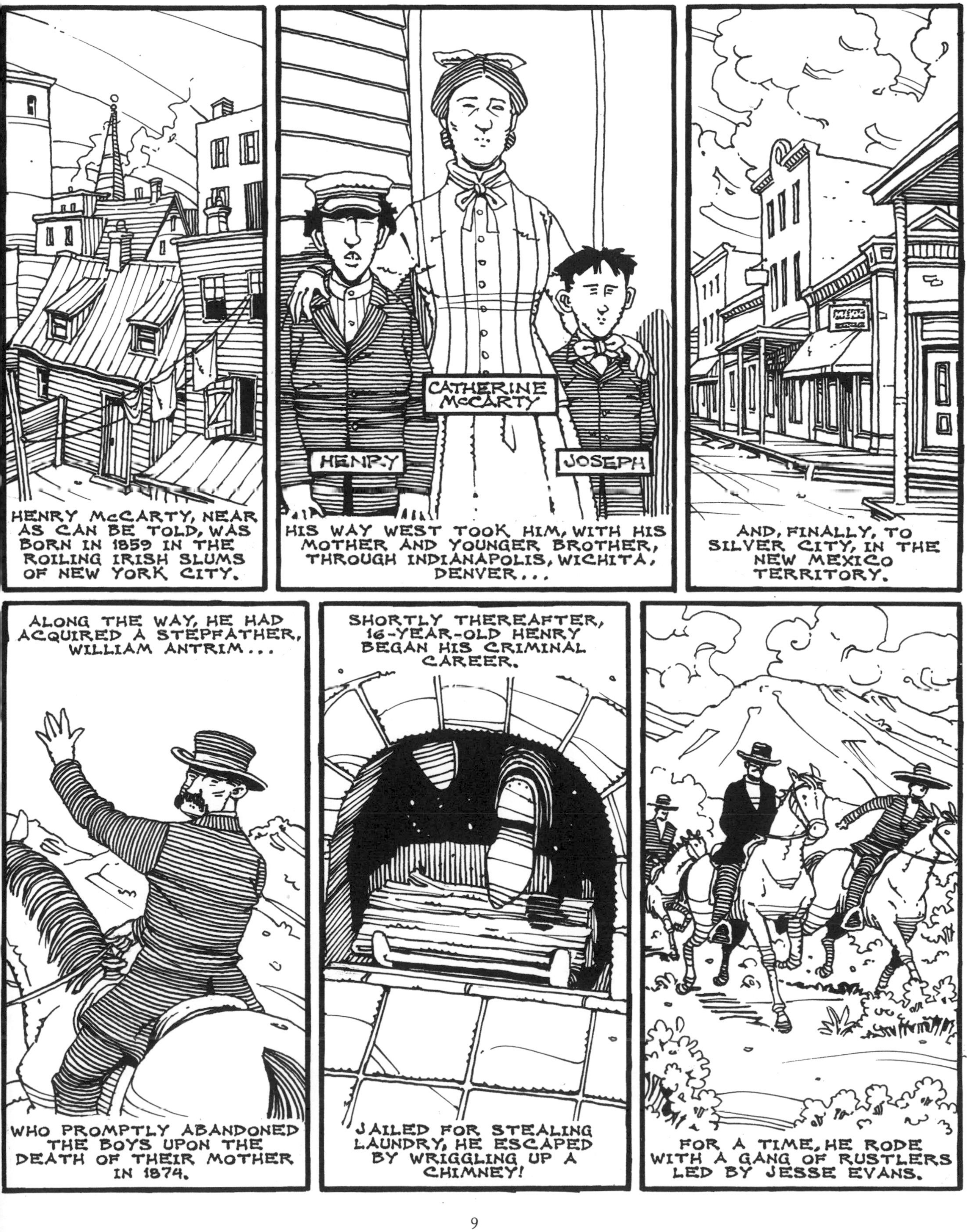
HENRY McCARTY, NEAR AS CAN BE TOLD, WAS BORN IN 1859 IN THE ROILING IRISH SLUMS OF NEW YORK CITY.
CATHERINE McCARTY
HENRY
JOSEPH
HIS WAY WEST TOOK HIM, WITH HIS MOTHER AND YOUNGER BROTHER, THROUGH INDIANAPOLIS, WICHITA, DENVER...
AND, FINALLY, TO SILVER CITY, IN THE NEW MEXICO TERRITORY.
ALONG THE WAY, HE HAD ACQUIRED A STEPFATHER, WILLIAM ANTRIM...
WHO PROMPTLY ABANDONED THE BOYS UPON THE DEATH OF THEIR MOTHER IN 1874.
SHORTLY THEREAFTER, 16-YEAR-OLD HENRY BEGAN HIS CRIMINAL CAREER.
JAILED FOR STEALING LAUNDRY, HE ESCAPED BY WRIGGLING UP A CHIMNEY!
FOR A TIME, HE RODE WITH A GANG OF RUSTLERS LED BY JESSE EVANS.

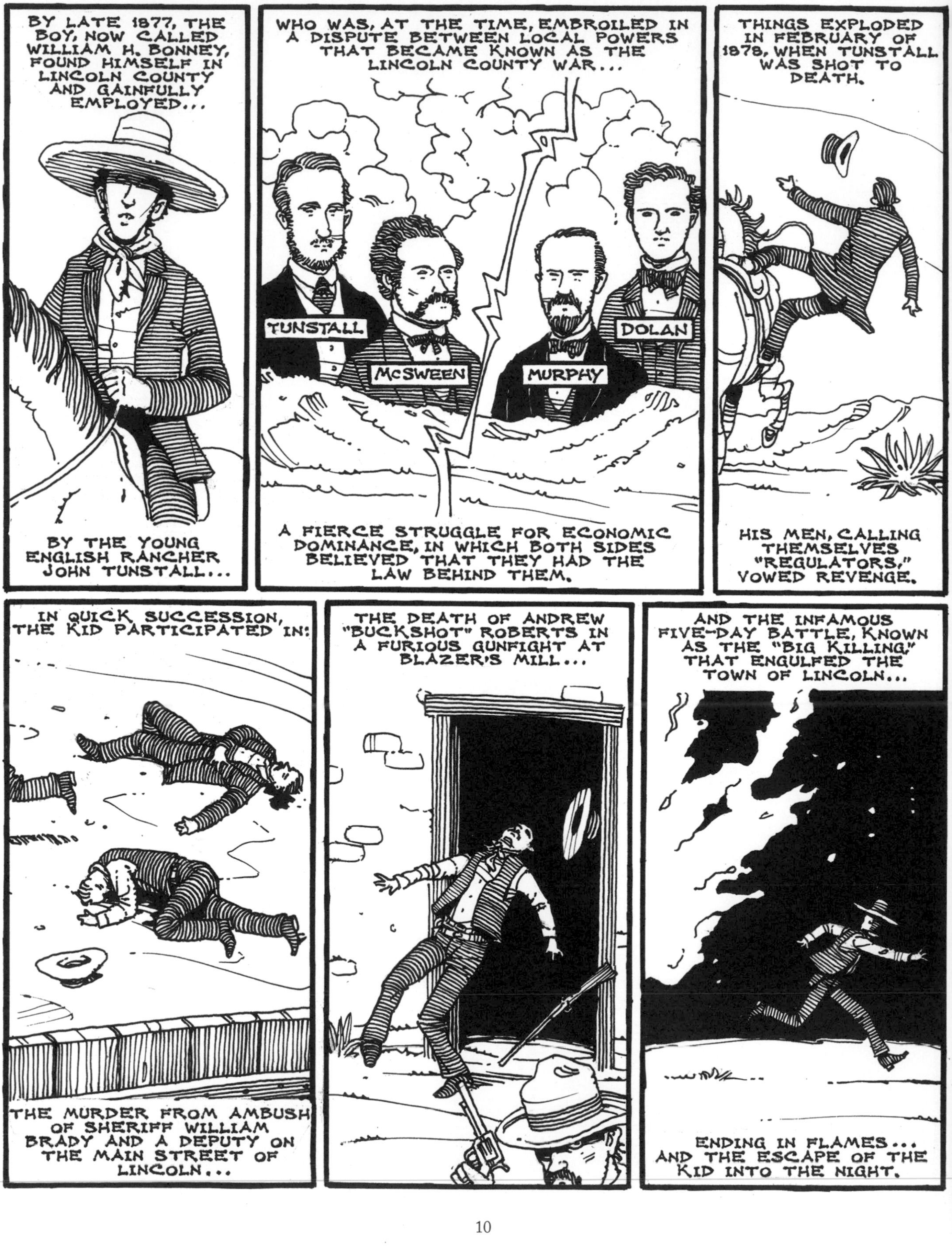
BY LATE 1877, THE BOY, NOW CALLED WILLIAM H. BONNEY, FOUND HIMSELF IN LINCOLN COUNTY AND GAINFULLY EMPLOYED...
BY THE YOUNG ENGLISH RANCHER JOHN TUNSTALL...
WHO WAS, AT THE TIME, EMBROILED IN A DISPUTE BETWEEN LOCAL POWERS THAT BECAME KNOWN AS THE LINCOLN COUNTY WAR...
TUNSTALL
McSWEEN
MURPHY
DOLAN
A FIERCE STRUGGLE FOR ECONOMIC DOMINANCE, IN WHICH BOTH SIDES BELIEVED THAT THEY HAD THE LAW BEHIND THEM.
THINGS EXPLODED IN FEBRUARY OF 1878, WHEN TUNSTALL WAS SHOT TO DEATH.
HIS MEN, CALLING THEMSELVES "REGULATORS," VOWED REVENGE.
IN QUICK SUCCESSION, THE KID PARTICIPATED IN:
THE MURDER FROM AMBUSH OF SHERIFF WILLIAM BRADY AND A DEPUTY ON THE MAIN STREET OF LINCOLN...
THE DEATH OF ANDREW "BUCKSHOT" ROBERTS IN A FURIOUS GUNFIGHT AT BLAZER'S MILL...
AND THE INFAMOUS FIVE-DAY BATTLE, KNOWN AS THE "BIG KILLING," THAT ENGULFED THE TOWN OF LINCOLN...
ENDING IN FLAMES... AND THE ESCAPE OF THE KID INTO THE NIGHT.

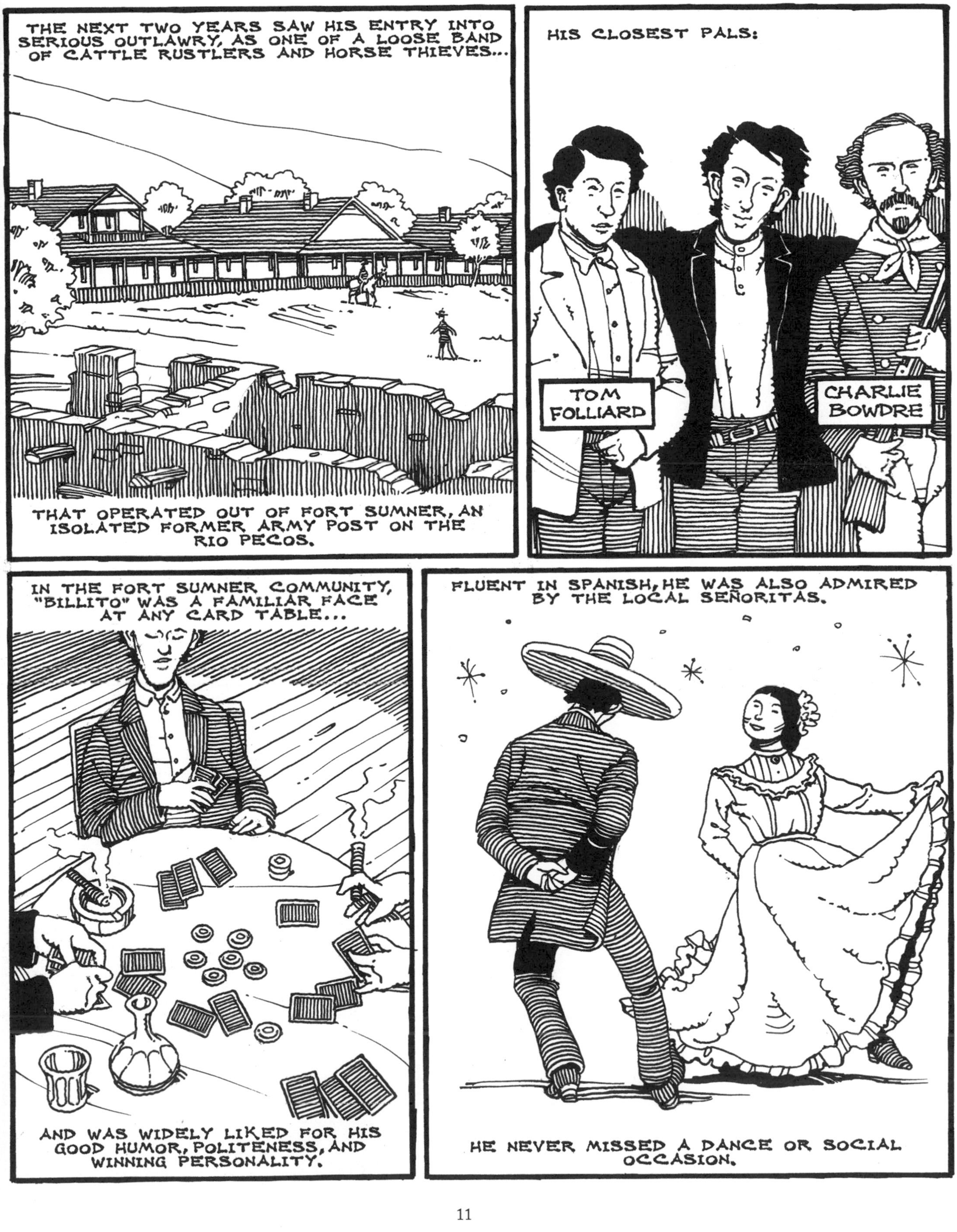
THE NEXT TWO YEARS SAW HIS ENTRY INTO SERIOUS OUTLAWRY, AS ONE OF A LOOSE BAND OF CATTLE RUSTLERS AND HORSE THIEVES...
THAT OPERATED OUT OF FORT SUMNER, AN ISOLATED FORMER ARMY POST ON THE RIO PECOS.
HIS CLOSEST PALS:
TOM FOLLIARD
CHARLIE BOWDRE
IN THE FORT SUMNER COMMUNITY, "BILLITO" WAS A FAMILIAR FACE AT ANY CARD TABLE...
AND WAS WIDELY LIKED FOR HIS GOOD HUMOR, POLITENESS, AND WINNING PERSONALITY.
FLUENT IN SPANISH, HE WAS ALSO ADMIRED BY THE LOCAL SEÑORITAS.
HE NEVER MISSED A DANCE OR SOCIAL OCCASION.

ANOTHER FAMILIAR PRESENCE IN TOWN WAS THE TOWERING RANCHER AND MERCHANT PAT GARRETT...

WHO, IN NOVEMBER OF 1880, WAS ELECTED SHERIFF OF LINCOLN COUNTY...

ON A PLATFORM THAT INCLUDED BRINGING TO JUSTICE THE KID AND HIS COHORTS.

IN THIS HE PROVED ABSOLUTELY RELENTLESS.

IN FACT, HE STARTED OUT BEFORE HE WAS SET TO TAKE OFFICE.

IN DECEMBER, AN AMBUSH AT FORT SUMNER RESULTED IN THE DEATH OF FOLLIARD...

AND THE ESCAPE OF THE KID WITH THREE COMPADRES.

FOUR DAYS LATER, THEY WERE TRACKED TO AN ABANDONED HOUSE TO THE EAST...

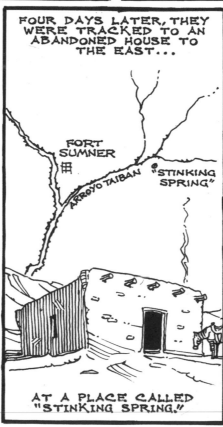

FORT SUMNER

ARROYO TAIBAN "STINKING SPRING"

AT A PLACE CALLED "STINKING SPRING."

A TWO-DAY STAND-OFF ENSUED, BOWDRE WAS KILLED...

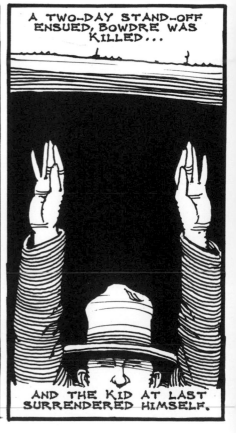

AND THE KID AT LAST SURRENDERED HIMSELF.

THE YOUNG OUTLAW LANGUISHED FOR THREE MONTHS IN THE JAIL AT SANTA FE, AWAITING TRIAL.

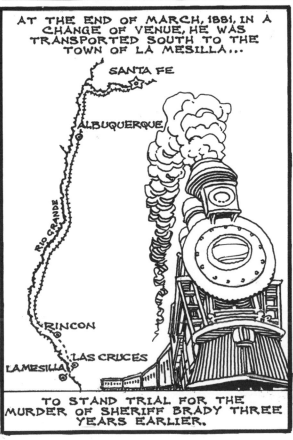

DURING THAT TIME, HE PENNED LETTER AFTER LETTER TO THE TERRITORIAL GOVERNOR, GENERAL LEW WALLACE...

DEMANDING THE PARDON THAT HE FELT CERTAIN WAS OWED HIM.

AT THE END OF MARCH, 1881, IN A CHANGE OF VENUE, HE WAS TRANSPORTED SOUTH TO THE TOWN OF LA MESILLA...

SANTA FE

ALBUQUERQUE

RIO GRANDE

RINCON

LAS CRUCES

LA MESILLA

TO STAND TRIAL FOR THE MURDER OF SHERIFF BRADY THREE YEARS EARLIER.

THE PROCEEDING, OF WHICH NO RECORD WAS KEPT, LASTED THREE DAYS...

AND ENDED WITH A VERDICT OF GUILTY.

THE SENTENCE WAS DEATH BY HANGING...

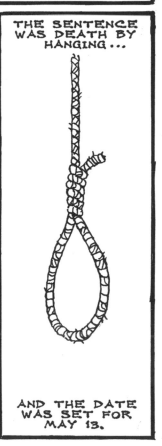

AND THE DATE WAS SET FOR MAY 13.

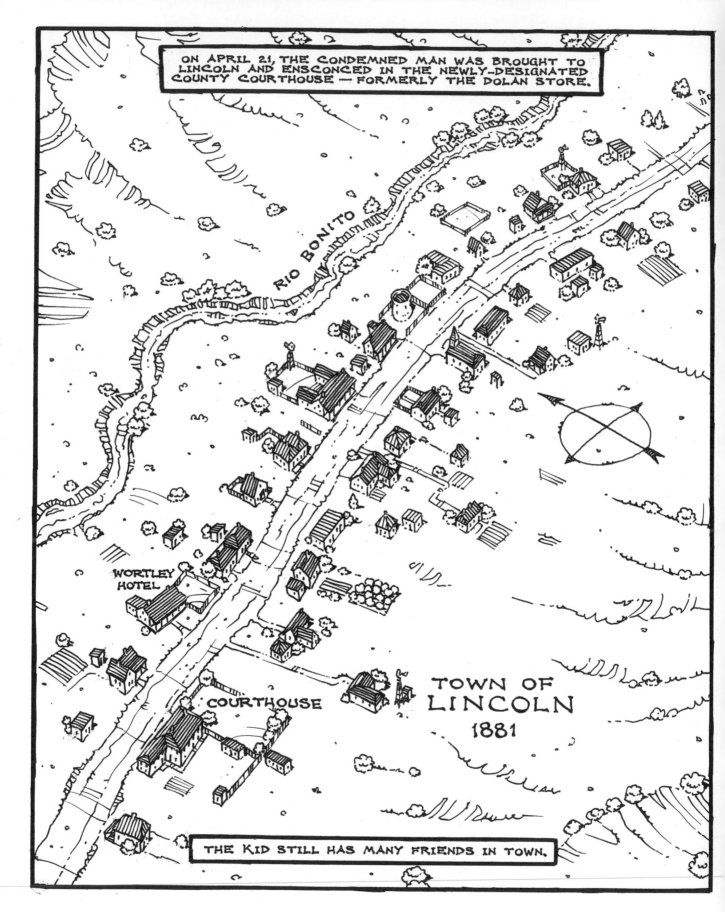

ON APRIL 21, THE CONDEMNED MAN WAS BROUGHT TO LINCOLN AND ENSCONCED IN THE NEWLY-DESIGNATED COUNTY COURTHOUSE — FORMERLY THE DOLAN STORE.

RIO BONITO

WORTLEY HOTEL

COURTHOUSE

TOWN OF LINCOLN 1881

THE KID STILL HAS MANY FRIENDS IN TOWN.

GARRETT HAS ASSIGNED TWO STALWART DEPUTIES TO WATCH OVER THE PRISONER DAY AND NIGHT:

BOB OLINGER

JAMES BELL

BELL PERFORMS HIS JOB WITH REASONABLE PROFESSIONALISM...

BUT BETWEEN OLINGER AND THE KID THERE IS POISONOUS FEELING GOING BACK YEARS.

WELL KNOWN AS AN UNPLEASANT CHARACTER, THE DEPUTY TAUNTS AND TORMENTS THE YOUNGER MAN AT EVERY OPPORTUNITY.

GO AHEAD... MAKE A BREAK FOR IT.

BOTH LAWMEN FEEL THAT THEY HAVE THE SITUATION FULLY UNDER THEIR CONTROL.

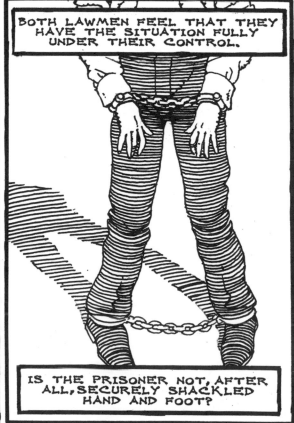

IS THE PRISONER NOT, AFTER ALL, SECURELY SHACKLED HAND AND FOOT?

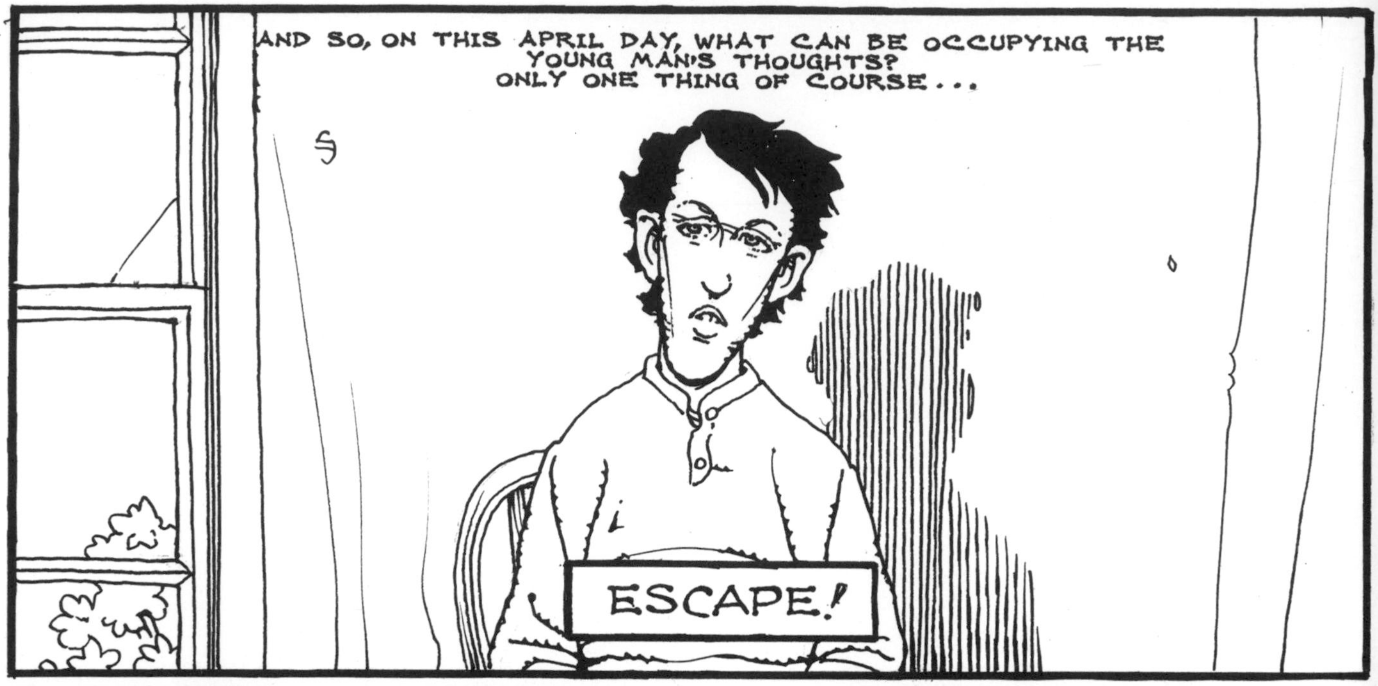
AND SO, ON THIS APRIL DAY, WHAT CAN BE OCCUPYING THE YOUNG MAN'S THOUGHTS? ONLY ONE THING OF COURSE...
ESCAPE!

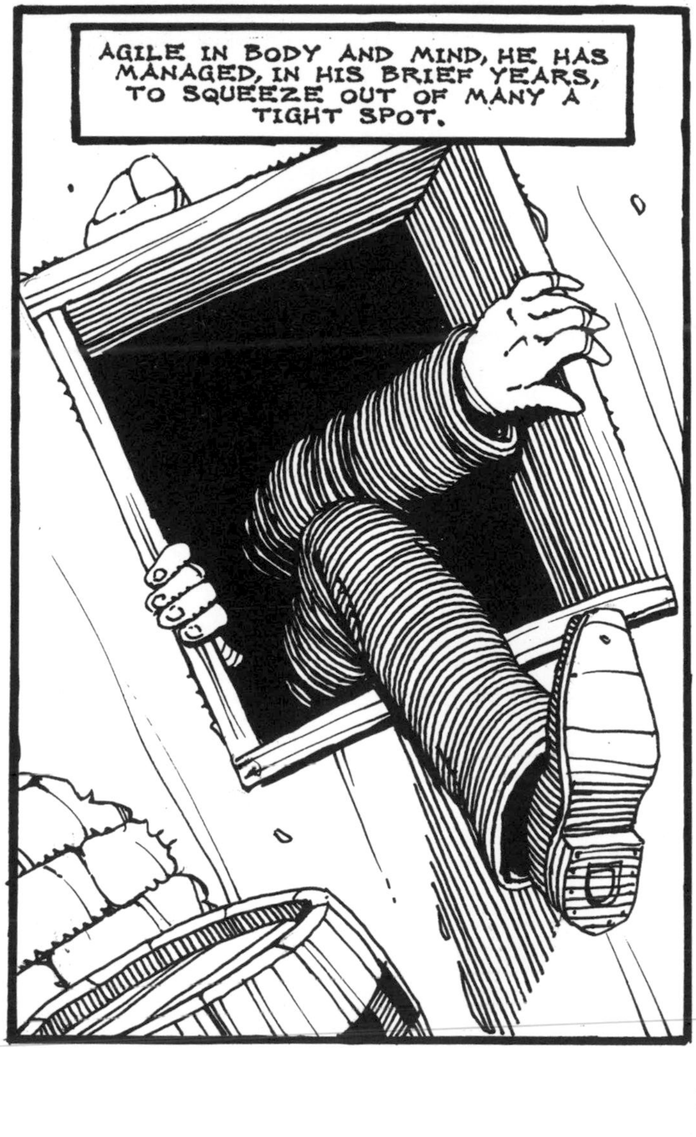
AGILE IN BODY AND MIND, HE HAS MANAGED, IN HIS BRIEF YEARS, TO SQUEEZE OUT OF MANY A TIGHT SPOT.

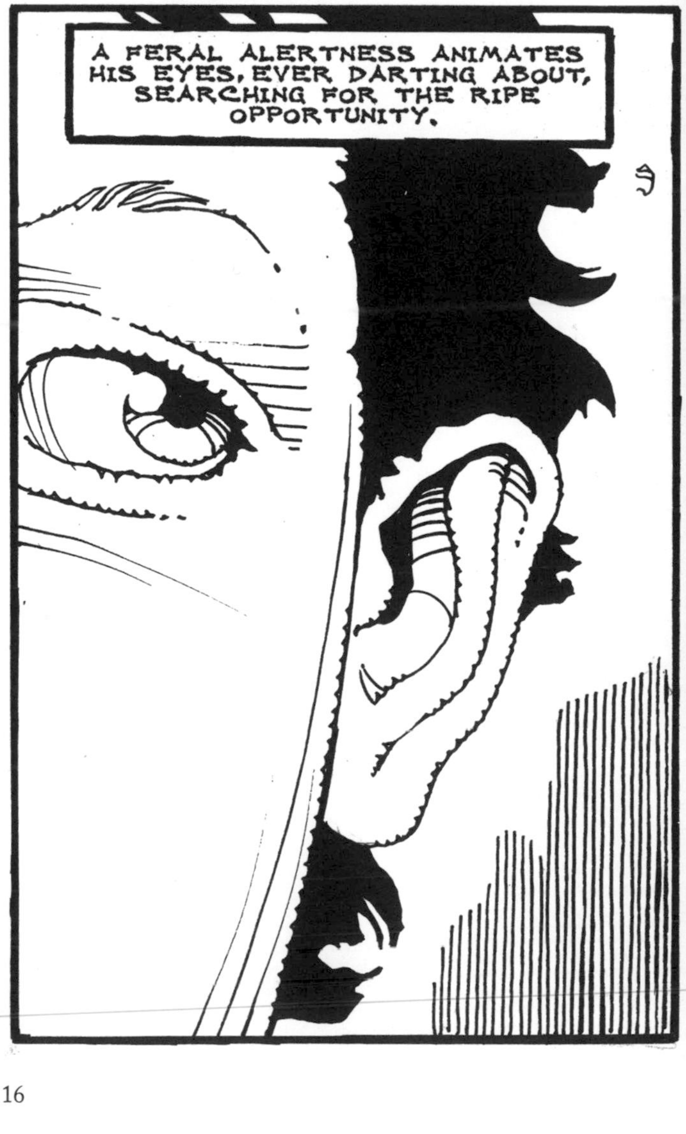
A FERAL ALERTNESS ANIMATES HIS EYES, EVER DARTING ABOUT, SEARCHING FOR THE RIPE OPPORTUNITY.

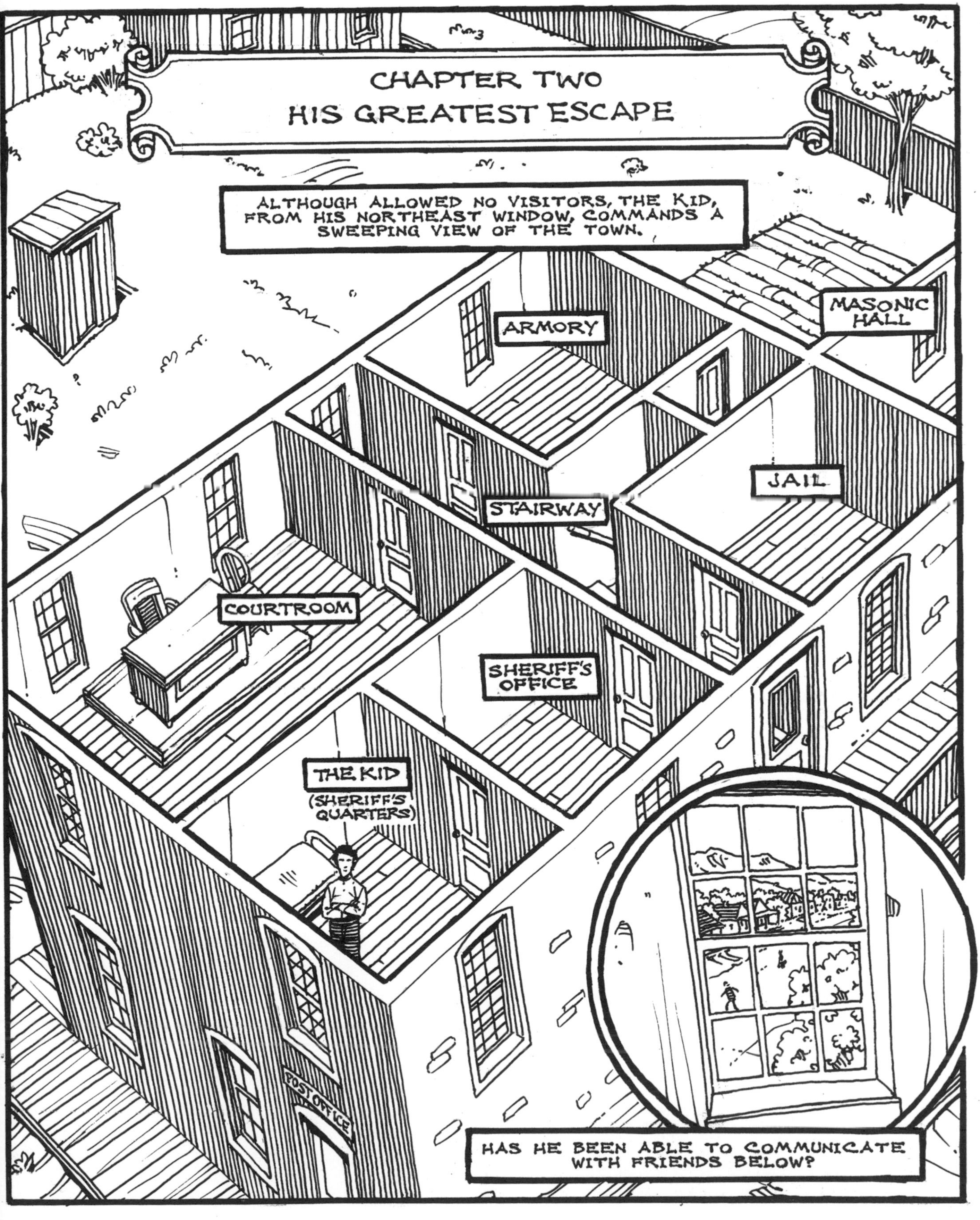
CHAPTER TWO
HIS GREATEST ESCAPE
ALTHOUGH ALLOWED NO VISITORS, THE KID, FROM HIS NORTHEAST WINDOW, COMMANDS A SWEEPING VIEW OF THE TOWN.
MASONIC HALL
ARMORY
JAIL
STAIRWAY
COURTROOM
SHERIFF'S OFFICE
THE KID
(SHERIFF'S QUARTERS)
POST OFFICE
HAS HE BEEN ABLE TO COMMUNICATE WITH FRIENDS BELOW?

THURSDAY, APRIL 28, 1881
AFTER A WEEK AT THE COURTHOUSE, HE HAS SURELY TAKEN NOTE OF THE DAILY ROUTINE.

BEING A HIGH-SECURITY CAPTIVE, HE RECEIVES MEALS IN HIS CELL...

WHILE THE COUNTY'S OTHER PRISONERS ARE TAKEN ACROSS THE STREET TO THE DINING ROOM OF THE WORTLEY HOTEL.

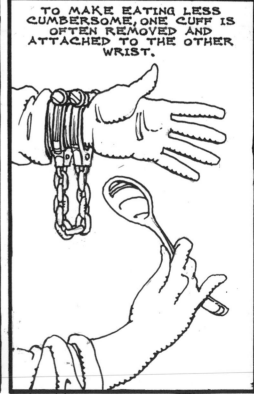

TO MAKE EATING LESS CUMBERSOME, ONE CUFF IS OFTEN REMOVED AND ATTACHED TO THE OTHER WRIST.

18

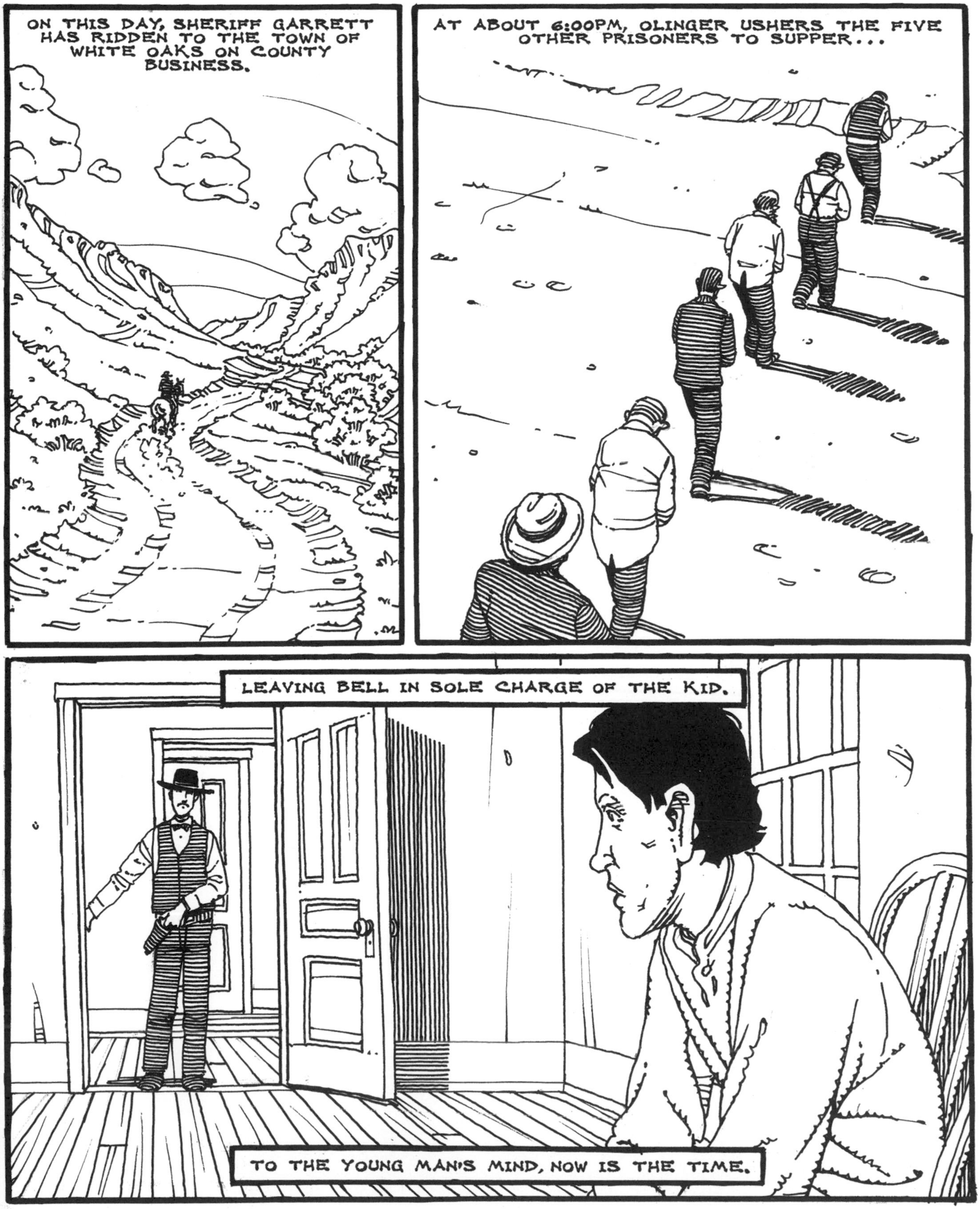
ON THIS DAY, SHERIFF GARRETT HAS RIDDEN TO THE TOWN OF WHITE OAKS ON COUNTY BUSINESS.
AT ABOUT 6:00PM, OLINGER USHERS THE FIVE OTHER PRISONERS TO SUPPER...
LEAVING BELL IN SOLE CHARGE OF THE KID.
TO THE YOUNG MAN'S MIND, NOW IS THE TIME.

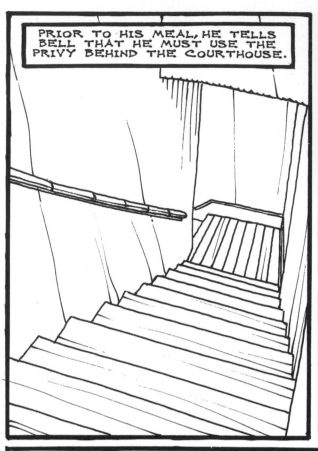

PRIOR TO HIS MEAL, HE TELLS BELL THAT HE MUST USE THE PRIVY BEHIND THE COURTHOUSE.

THEY DESCEND THE STAIRS AND EMERGE VIA THE REAR DOOR.

BELL WAITS WHILE THE PRISONER DOES HIS "BUSINESS."

WAS ONE OF HIS WRISTS UNCUFFED FOR THIS?

THE DEPUTY THEN WALKS THE KID BACK INSIDE AND UP THE STAIRS.

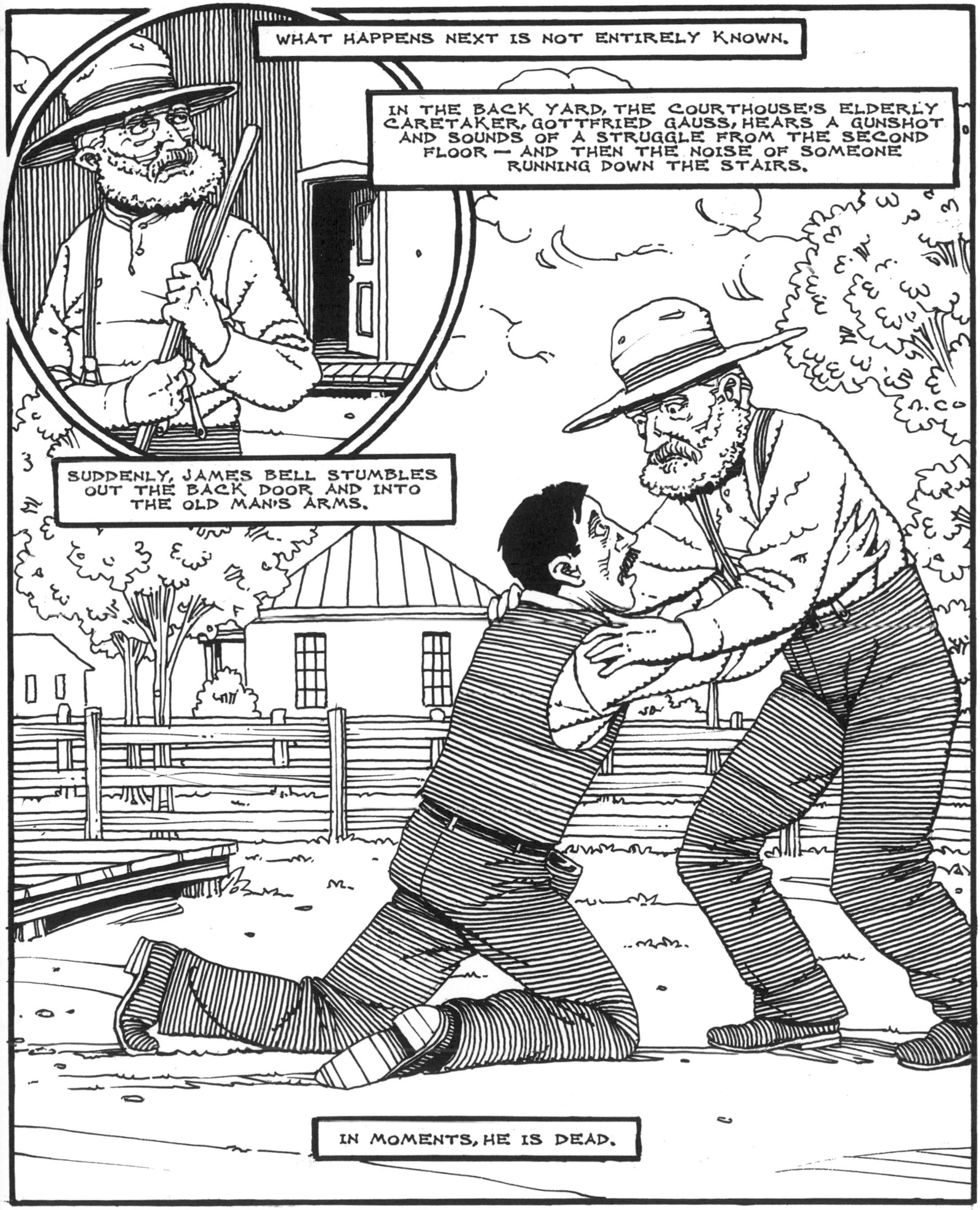
WHAT HAPPENS NEXT IS NOT ENTIRELY KNOWN.
IN THE BACK YARD, THE COURTHOUSE'S ELDERLY CARETAKER, GOTTFRIED GAUSS, HEARS A GUNSHOT AND SOUNDS OF A STRUGGLE FROM THE SECOND FLOOR — AND THEN THE NOISE OF SOMEONE RUNNING DOWN THE STAIRS.
SUDDENLY, JAMES BELL STUMBLES OUT THE BACK DOOR AND INTO THE OLD MAN'S ARMS.
IN MOMENTS, HE IS DEAD.

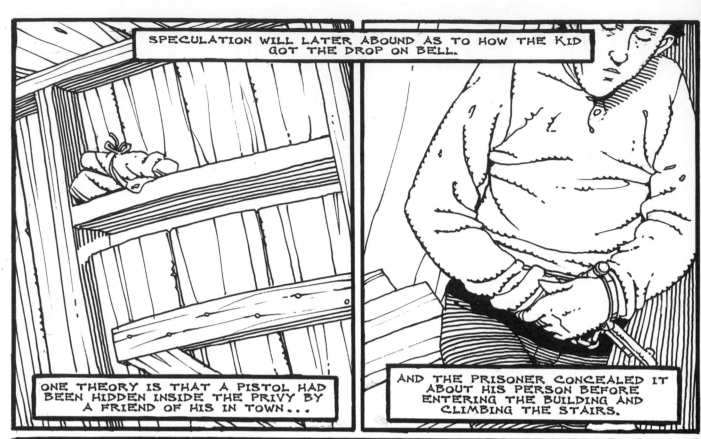

SPECULATION WILL LATER ABOUND AS TO HOW THE KID GOT THE DROP ON BELL.

ONE THEORY IS THAT A PISTOL HAD BEEN HIDDEN INSIDE THE PRIVY BY A FRIEND OF HIS IN TOWN...

AND THE PRISONER CONCEALED IT ABOUT HIS PERSON BEFORE ENTERING THE BUILDING AND CLIMBING THE STAIRS.

HOW THE DEPUTY COULD HAVE MISSED SEEING IT IS NOT CERTAIN.

OBVIOUSLY HE IS FATALLY INATTENTIVE ON THIS DAY.

IN ANOTHER HYPOTHESIS, BELL LAGS BEHIND ON THE STAIRS, ALLOWING THE KID TO SLIP AROUND THE CORNER AND AMBUSH HIM...

BY A BLOW TO THE HEAD WITH HIS HANDCUFFS.

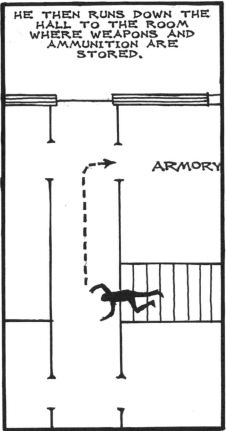

HE THEN RUNS DOWN THE HALL TO THE ROOM WHERE WEAPONS AND AMMUNITION ARE STORED.

ARMORY

THERE, HE FINDS THE NECESSARY FIREARM...

AND RUSHES BACK TO FINISH OFF THE DEPUTY AS HE BOUNDS DOWN THE STAIRS.

YET A THIRD SCENARIO HAS THE KID AGAIN STUNNING BELL WITH HIS CUFFS.

THE TWO THEN WRESTLE ON THE FLOOR, ENABLING HIM TO SNATCH AWAY THE LAWMAN'S GUN.

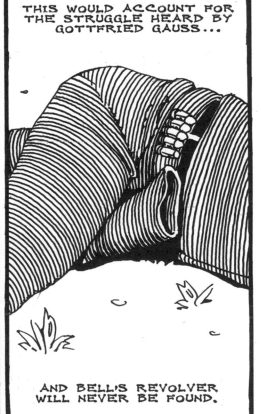

THIS WOULD ACCOUNT FOR THE STRUGGLE HEARD BY GOTTFRIED GAUSS...

AND BELL'S REVOLVER WILL NEVER BE FOUND.

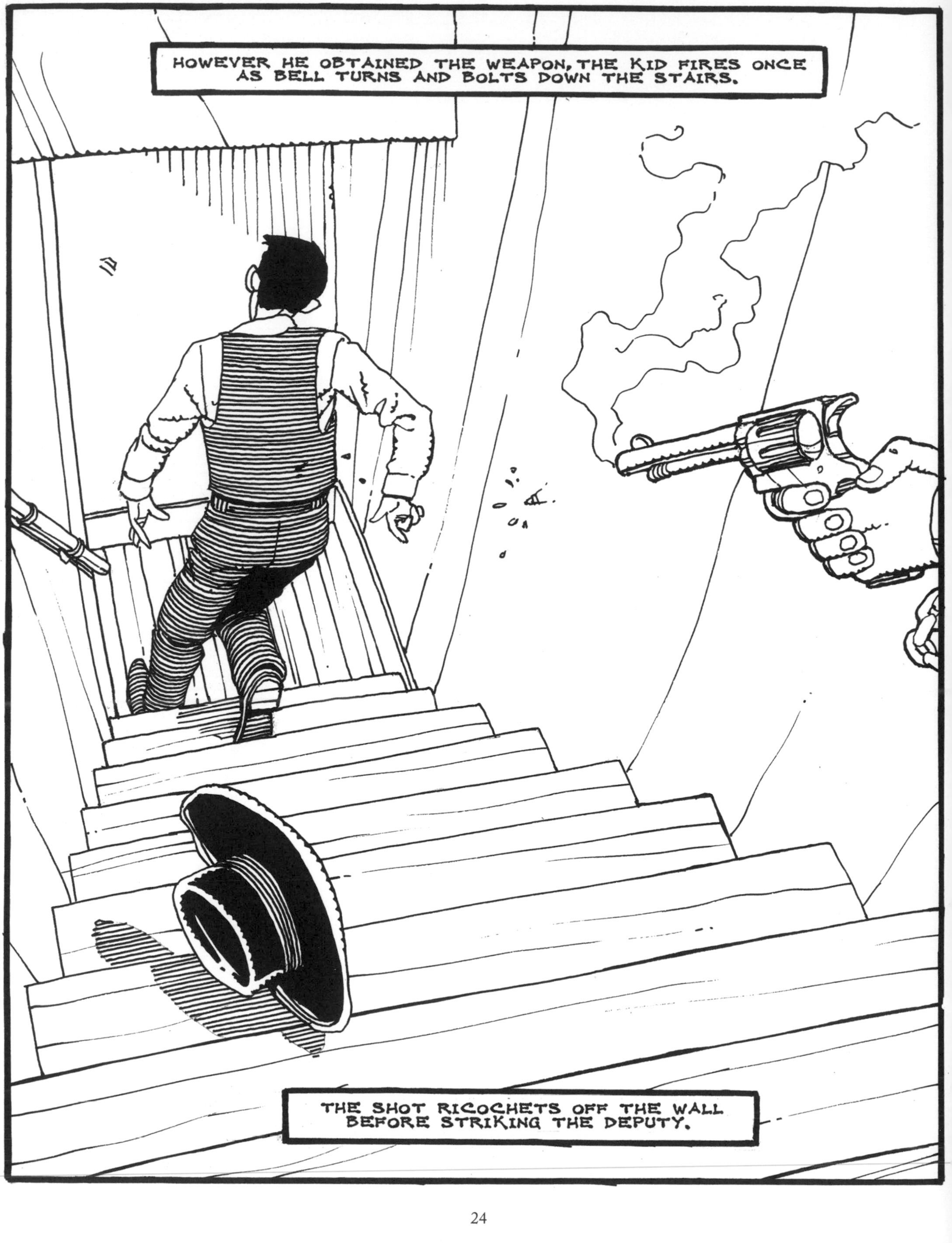
HOWEVER HE OBTAINED THE WEAPON, THE KID FIRES ONCE AS BELL TURNS AND BOLTS DOWN THE STAIRS.
THE SHOT RICOCHETS OFF THE WALL BEFORE STRIKING THE DEPUTY.

OVER AT THE WORTLEY, OLINGER HAS HEARD THE SHOT AND KNOWS AT ONCE WHAT'S UP.

HE HERDS HIS PRISONERS OUTSIDE...

AND STRIDES ACROSS THE ROAD TO THE COURTHOUSE.

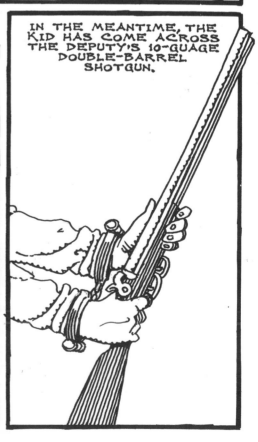

IN THE MEANTIME, THE KID HAS COME ACROSS THE DEPUTY'S 10-GUAGE DOUBLE-BARREL SHOTGUN.

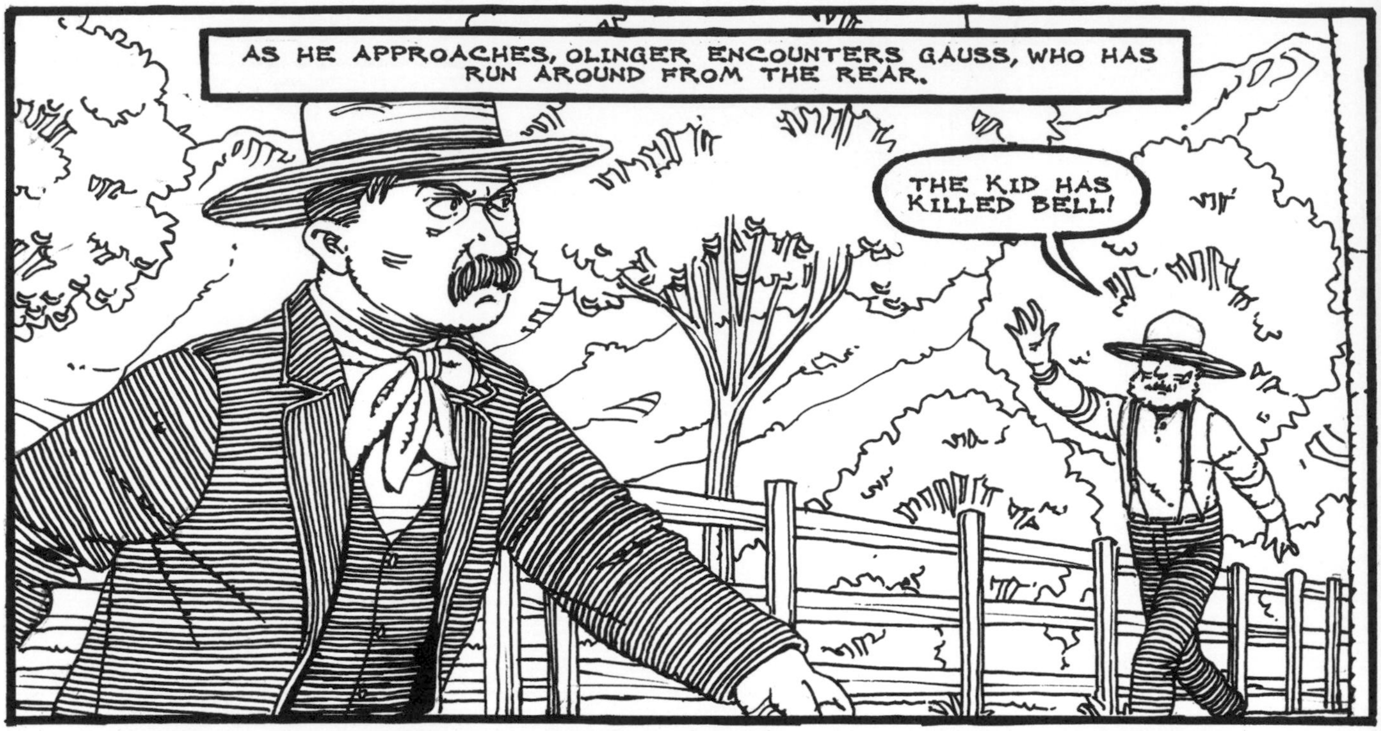
AS HE APPROACHES, OLINGER ENCOUNTERS GAUSS, WHO HAS RUN AROUND FROM THE REAR.
THE KID HAS KILLED BELL!

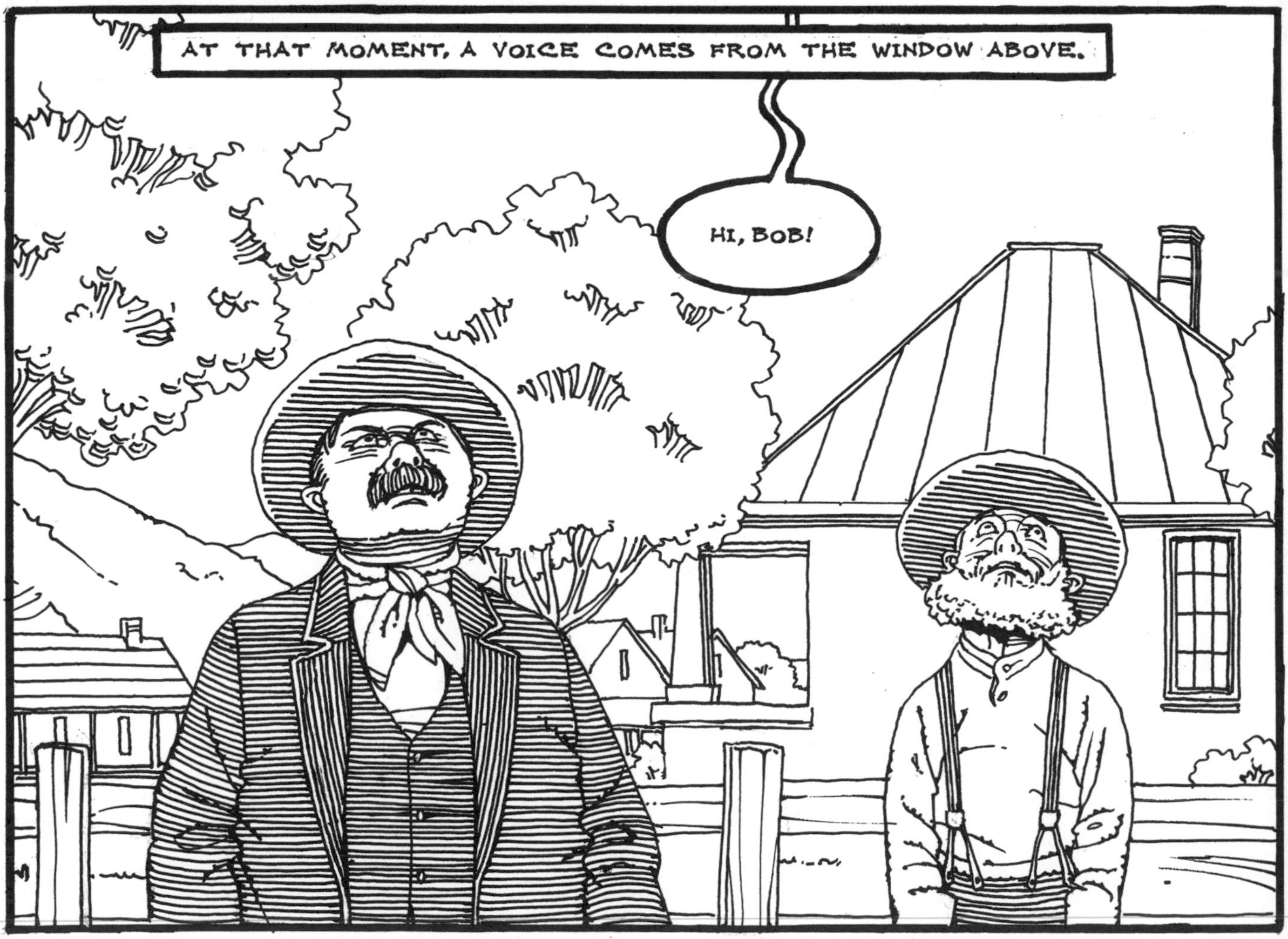
AT THAT MOMENT, A VOICE COMES FROM THE WINDOW ABOVE.
HI, BOB!

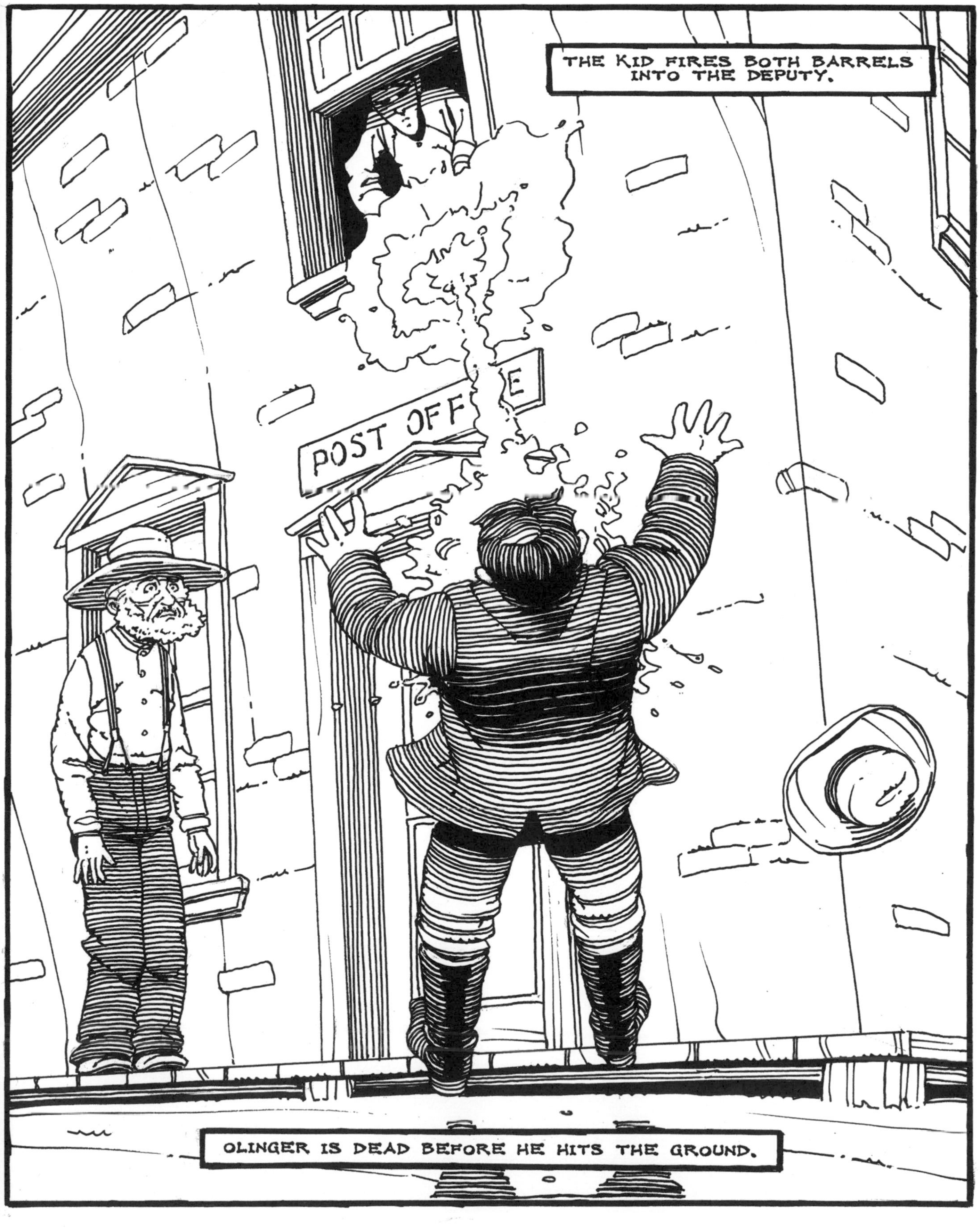
THE KID FIRES BOTH BARRELS INTO THE DEPUTY.
POST OFF E
OLINGER IS DEAD BEFORE HE HITS THE GROUND.

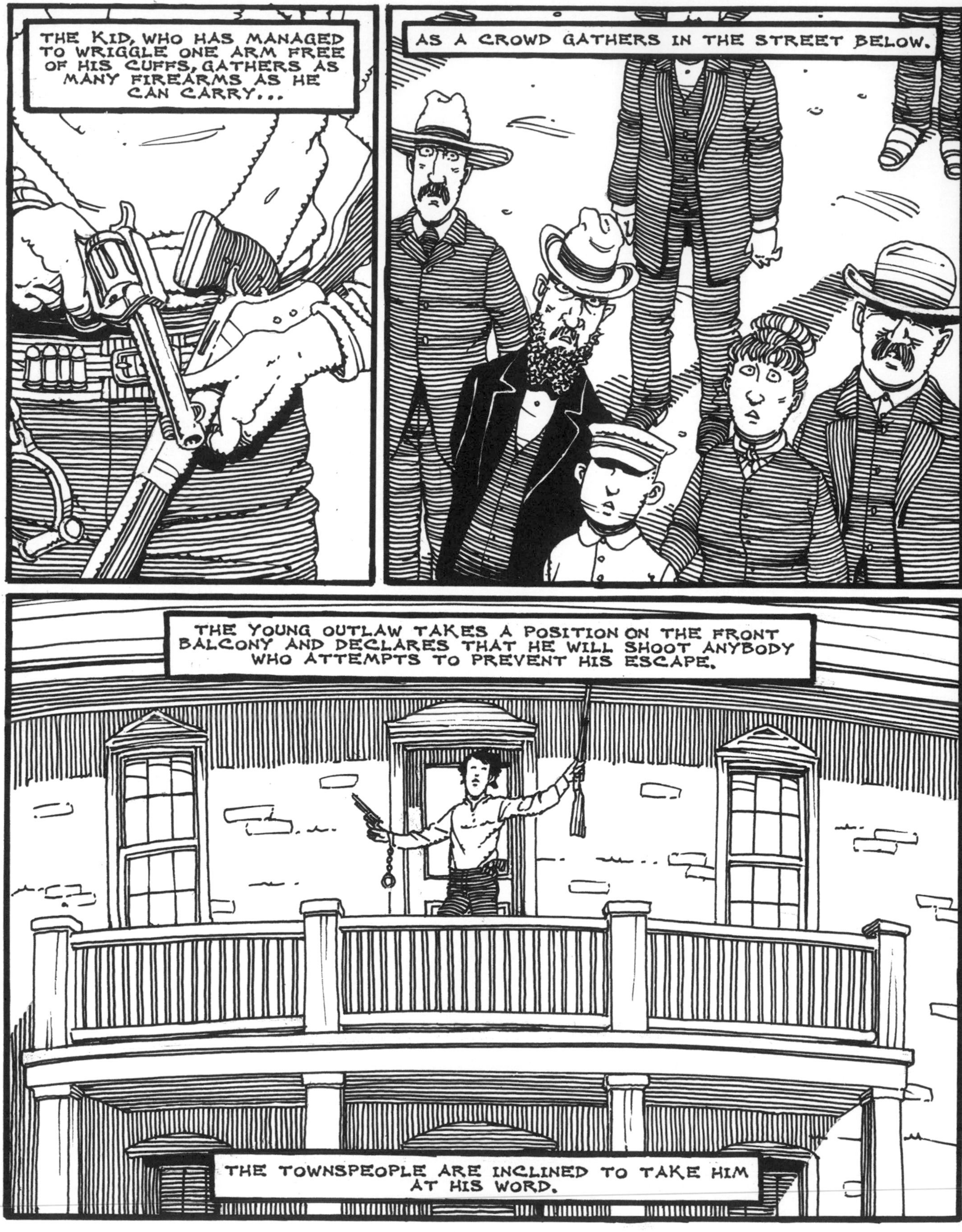
THE KID, WHO HAS MANAGED TO WRIGGLE ONE ARM FREE OF HIS CUFFS, GATHERS AS MANY FIREARMS AS HE CAN CARRY...
AS A CROWD GATHERS IN THE STREET BELOW.
THE YOUNG OUTLAW TAKES A POSITION ON THE FRONT BALCONY AND DECLARES THAT HE WILL SHOOT ANYBODY WHO ATTEMPTS TO PREVENT HIS ESCAPE.
THE TOWNSPEOPLE ARE INCLINED TO TAKE HIM AT HIS WORD.

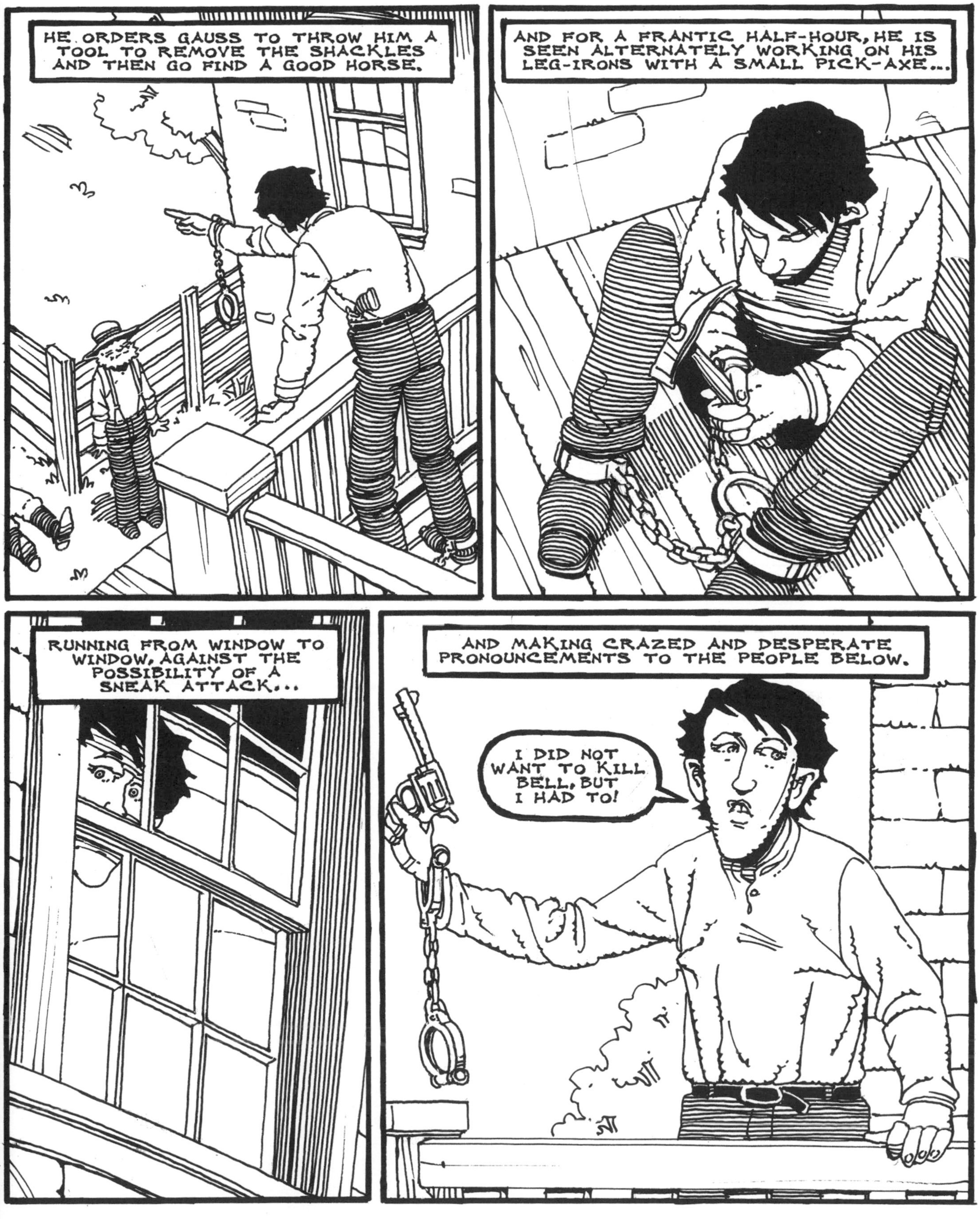
HE ORDERS GAUSS TO THROW HIM A TOOL TO REMOVE THE SHACKLES AND THEN GO FIND A GOOD HORSE.
AND FOR A FRANTIC HALF-HOUR, HE IS SEEN ALTERNATELY WORKING ON HIS LEG-IRONS WITH A SMALL PICK-AXE...
RUNNING FROM WINDOW TO WINDOW, AGAINST THE POSSIBILITY OF A SNEAK ATTACK...
AND MAKING CRAZED AND DESPERATE PRONOUNCEMENTS TO THE PEOPLE BELOW.
I DID NOT WANT TO KILL BELL, BUT I HAD TO!

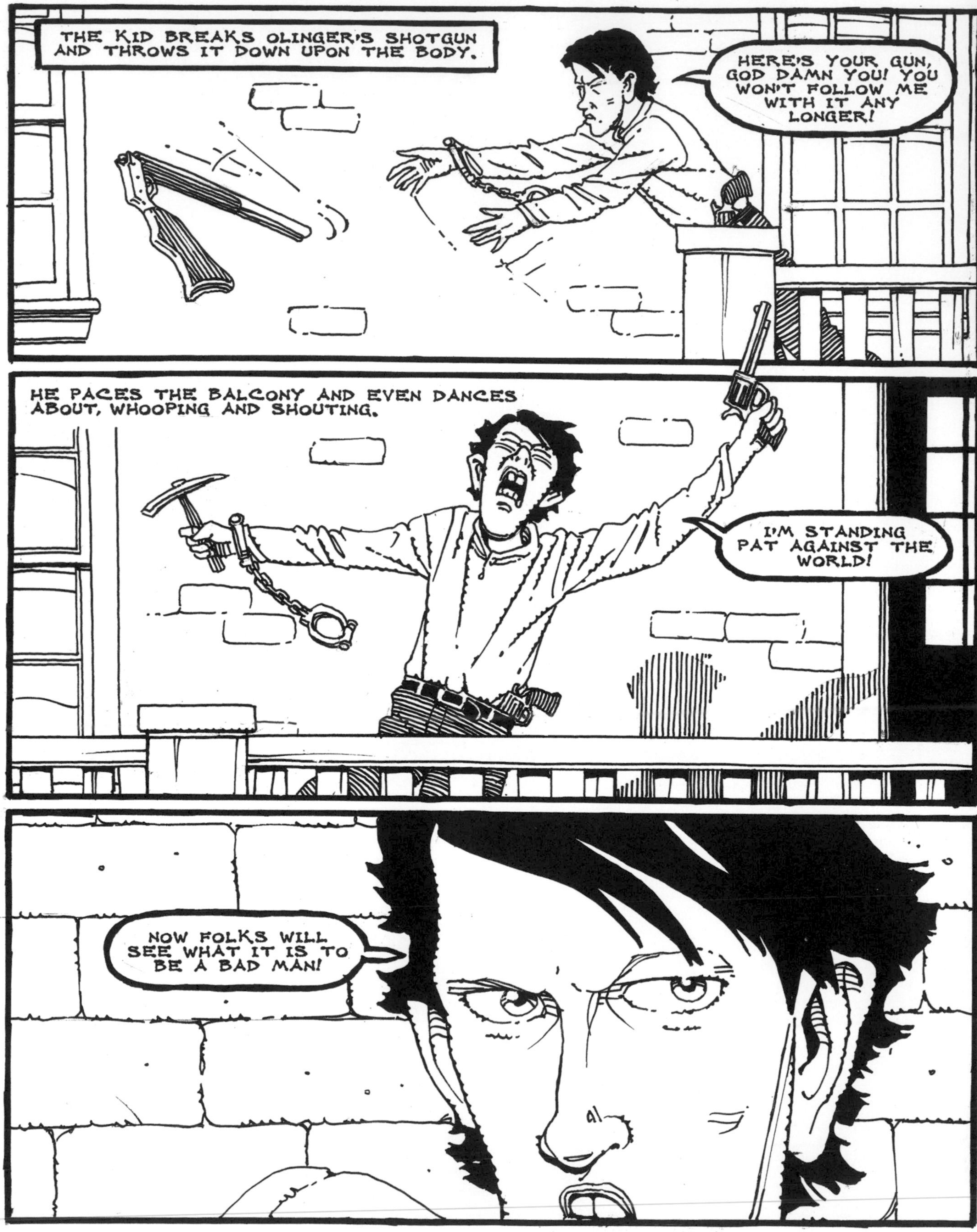
THE KID BREAKS OLINGER'S SHOTGUN AND THROWS IT DOWN UPON THE BODY.
HERE'S YOUR GUN, GOD DAMN YOU! YOU WON'T FOLLOW ME WITH IT ANY LONGER!
HE PACES THE BALCONY AND EVEN DANCES ABOUT, WHOOPING AND SHOUTING.
I'M STANDING PAT AGAINST THE WORLD!
NOW FOLKS WILL SEE WHAT IT IS TO BE A BAD MAN!

THE KID AT LAST HAS WORKED ONE FOOT FROM THE LEG IRONS AND LOOPS THE LOOSE END OF CHAIN OVER HIS BELT.

AS THE SUN GOES DOWN, HE EMERGES FROM THE BACK OF THE COURTHOUSE, WHERE GAUSS HAS BROUGHT A HORSE "BORROWED" FROM THE TOWN CORRAL.

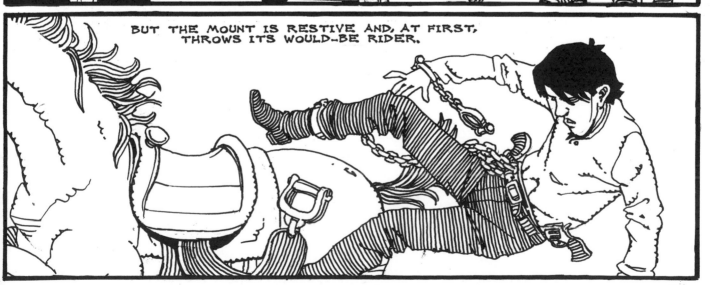

BUT THE MOUNT IS RESTIVE AND, AT FIRST, THROWS ITS WOULD-BE RIDER.

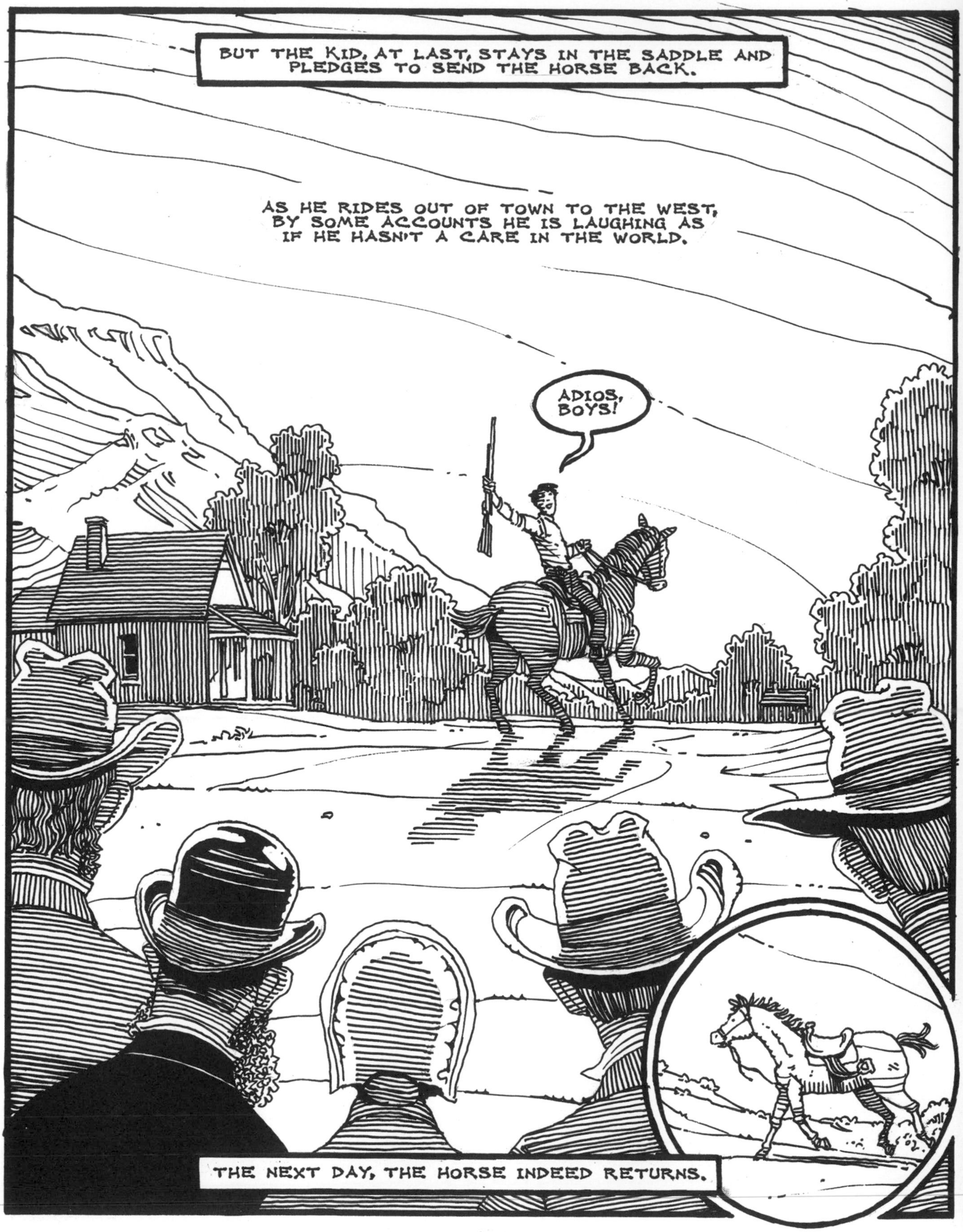
BUT THE KID, AT LAST, STAYS IN THE SADDLE AND PLEDGES TO SEND THE HORSE BACK.
AS HE RIDES OUT OF TOWN TO THE WEST, BY SOME ACCOUNTS HE IS LAUGHING AS IF HE HASN'T A CARE IN THE WORLD.
ADIOS, BOYS!
THE NEXT DAY, THE HORSE INDEED RETURNS.

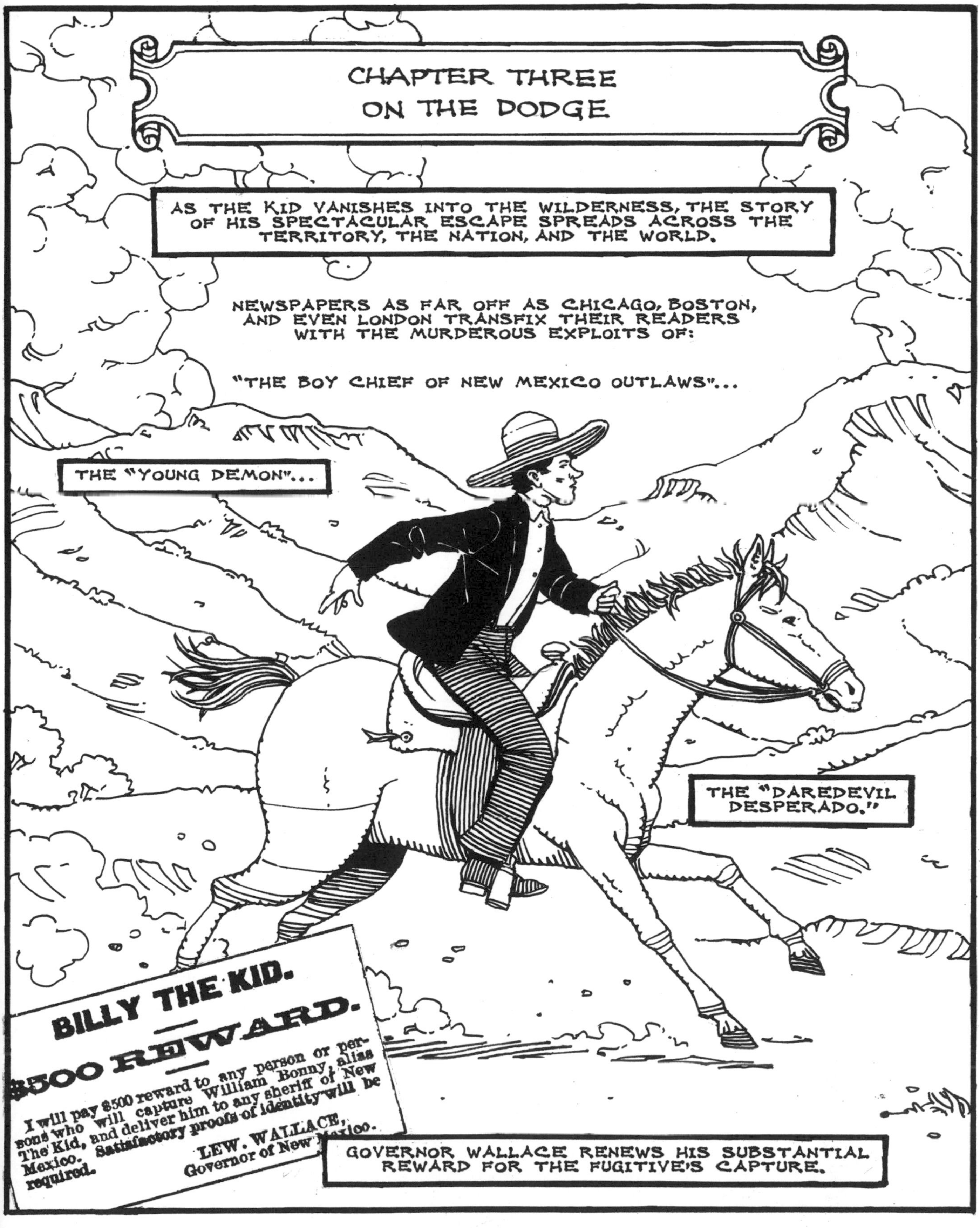
CHAPTER THREE
ON THE DODGE
AS THE KID VANISHES INTO THE WILDERNESS, THE STORY OF HIS SPECTACULAR ESCAPE SPREADS ACROSS THE TERRITORY, THE NATION, AND THE WORLD.
NEWSPAPERS AS FAR OFF AS CHICAGO, BOSTON, AND EVEN LONDON TRANSFIX THEIR READERS WITH THE MURDEROUS EXPLOITS OF:
"THE BOY CHIEF OF NEW MEXICO OUTLAWS"...
THE "YOUNG DEMON"...
THE "DAREDEVIL DESPERADO."
BILLY THE KID.
$500 REWARD.
I will pay $500 reward to any person or persons who will capture William Bonny, alias The Kid, and deliver him to any sheriff of New Mexico. Satisfactory proofs of identity will be required.
LEW. WALLACE, Governor of New Mexico.
GOVERNOR WALLACE RENEWS HIS SUBSTANTIAL REWARD FOR THE FUGITIVE'S CAPTURE.

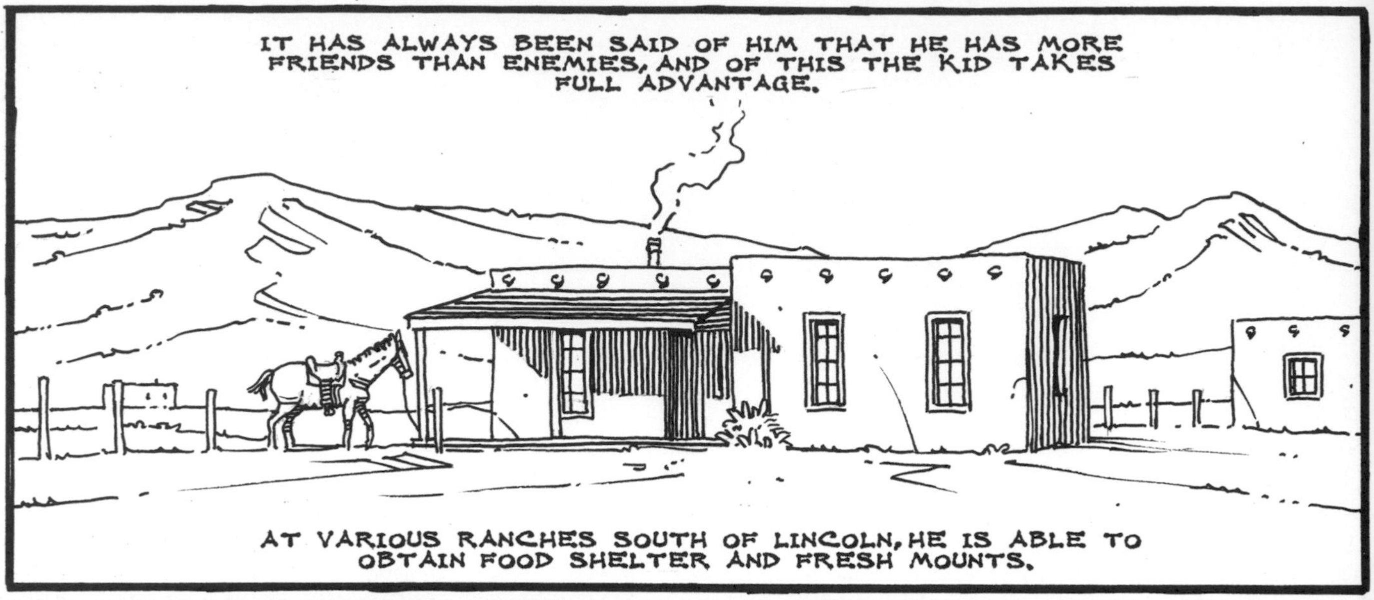
IT HAS ALWAYS BEEN SAID OF HIM THAT HE HAS MORE FRIENDS THAN ENEMIES, AND OF THIS THE KID TAKES FULL ADVANTAGE.
AT VARIOUS RANCHES SOUTH OF LINCOLN, HE IS ABLE TO OBTAIN FOOD SHELTER AND FRESH MOUNTS.

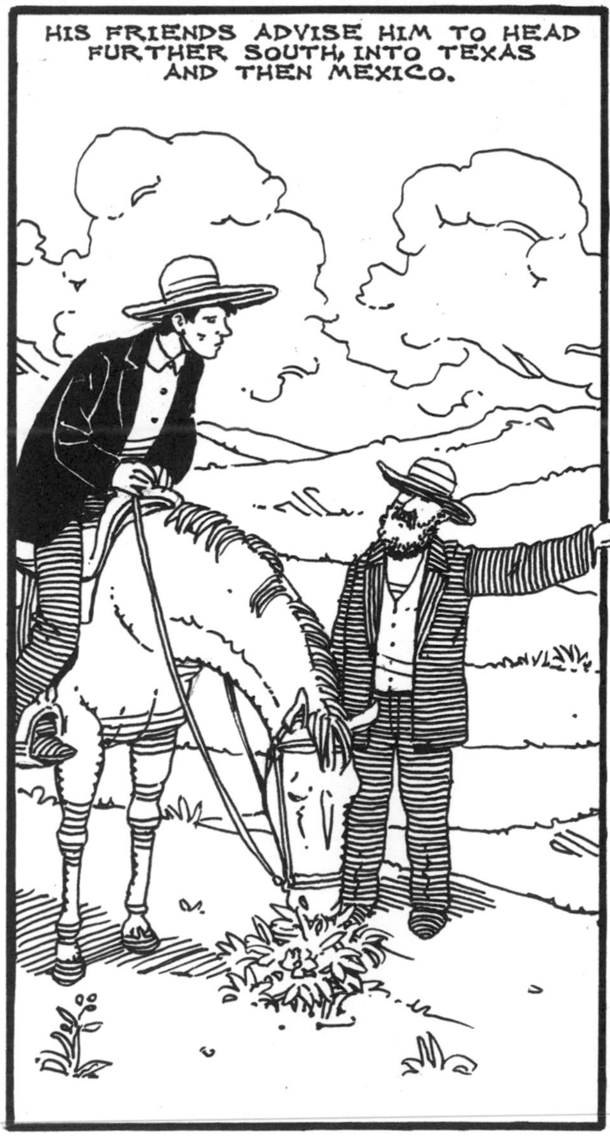
HIS FRIENDS ADVISE HIM TO HEAD FURTHER SOUTH, INTO TEXAS AND THEN MEXICO.

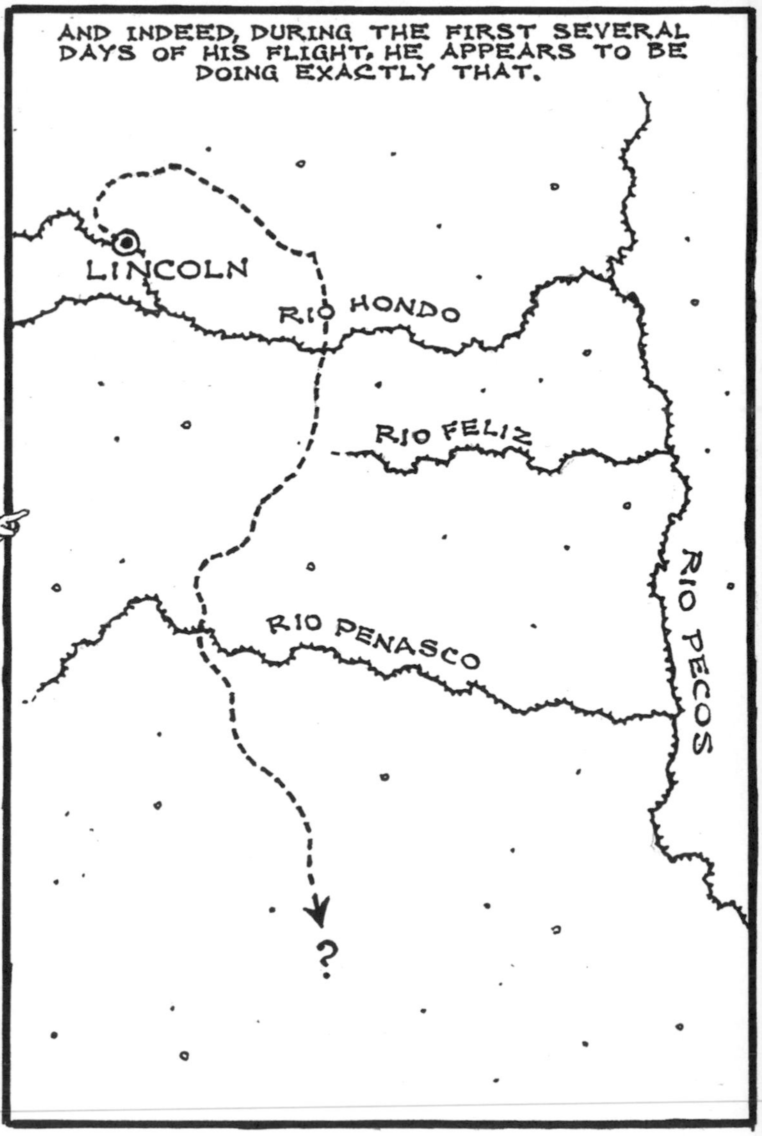
AND INDEED, DURING THE FIRST SEVERAL DAYS OF HIS FLIGHT, HE APPEARS TO BE DOING EXACTLY THAT.
LINCOLN
RIO HONDO
RIO FELIZ
RIO PENASCO
RIO PECOS
?

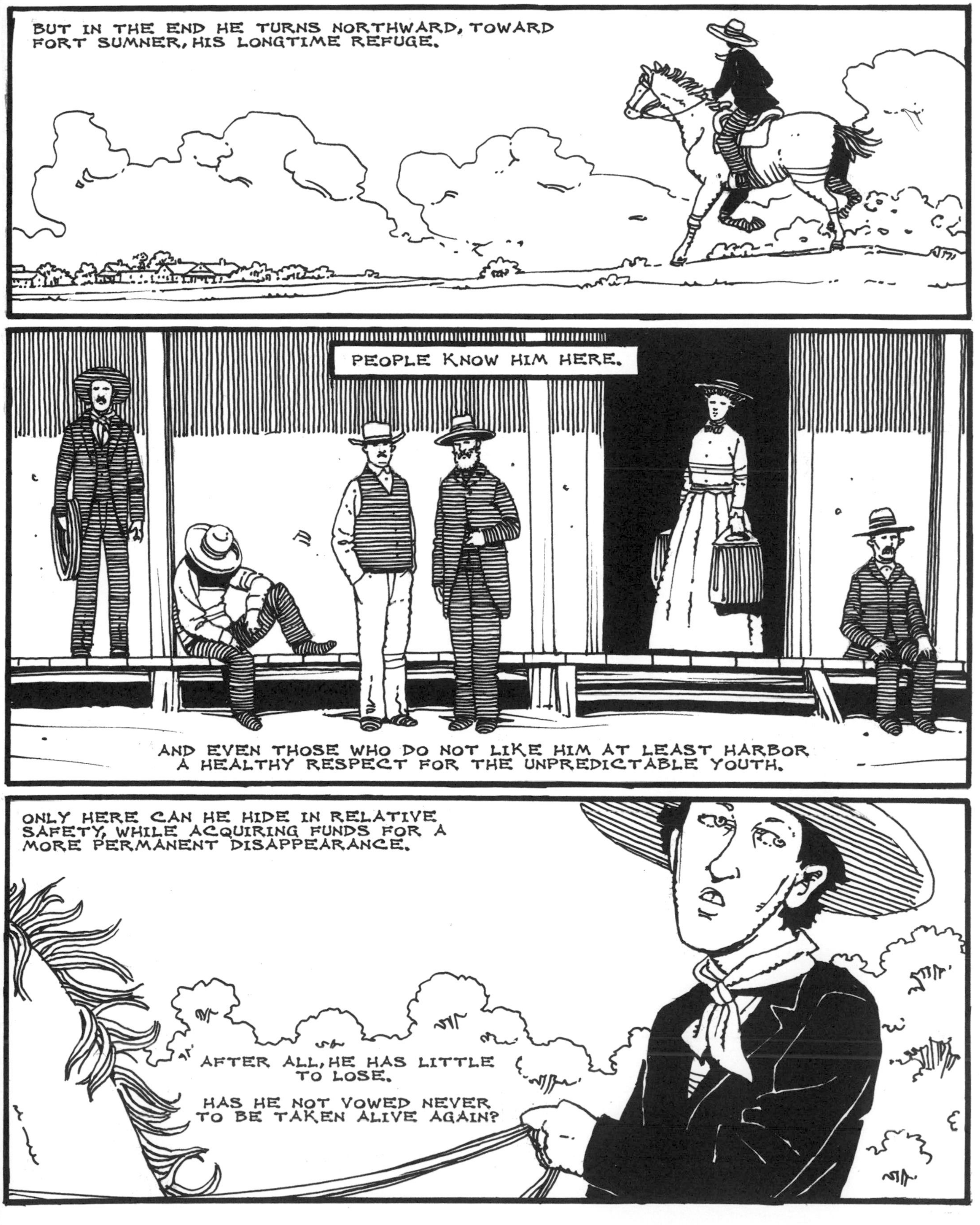
BUT IN THE END HE TURNS NORTHWARD, TOWARD FORT SUMNER, HIS LONGTIME REFUGE.
PEOPLE KNOW HIM HERE.
AND EVEN THOSE WHO DO NOT LIKE HIM AT LEAST HARBOR A HEALTHY RESPECT FOR THE UNPREDICTABLE YOUTH.
ONLY HERE CAN HE HIDE IN RELATIVE SAFETY, WHILE ACQUIRING FUNDS FOR A MORE PERMANENT DISAPPEARANCE.
AFTER ALL, HE HAS LITTLE TO LOSE.
HAS HE NOT VOWED NEVER TO BE TAKEN ALIVE AGAIN?

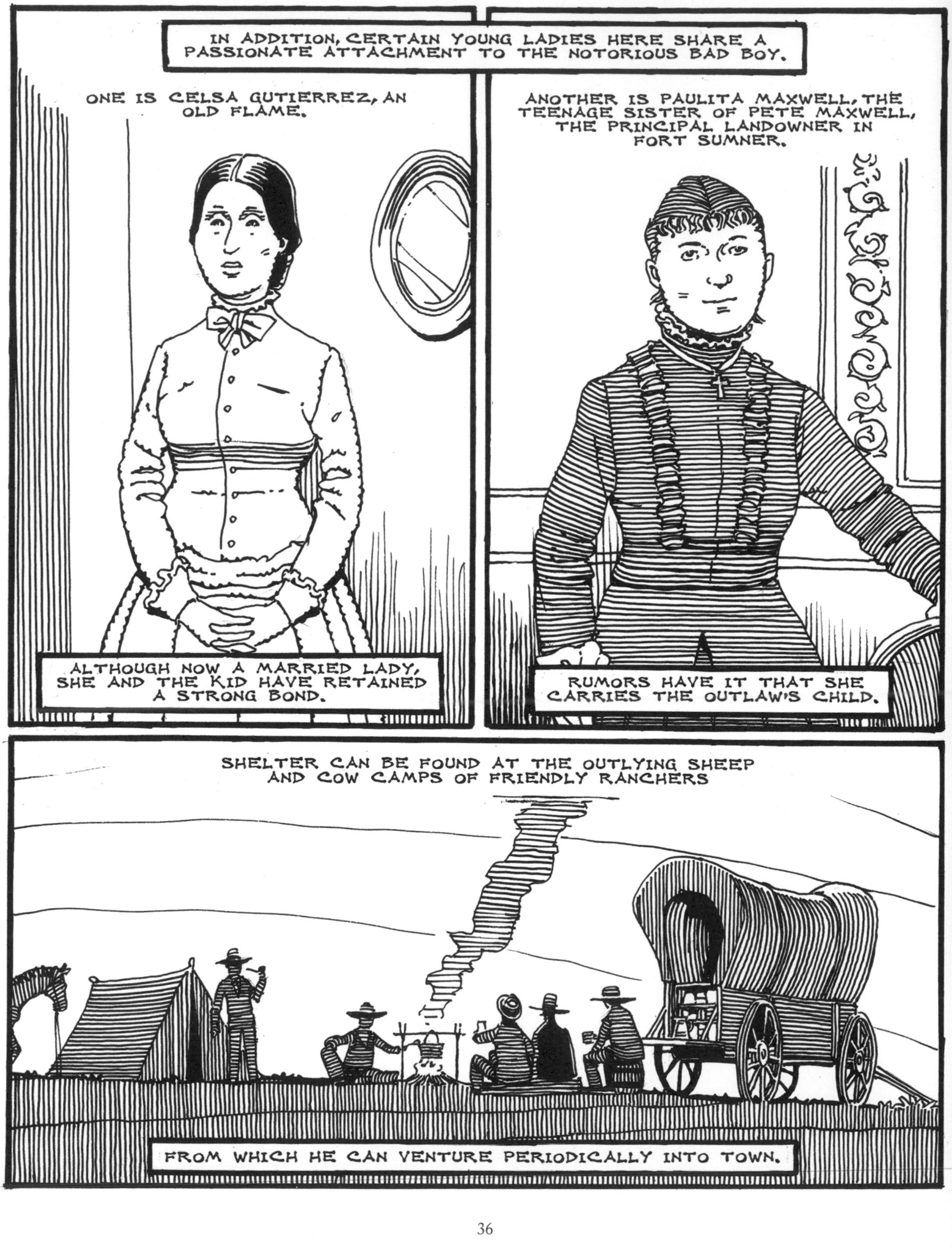
IN ADDITION, CERTAIN YOUNG LADIES HERE SHARE A PASSIONATE ATTACHMENT TO THE NOTORIOUS BAD BOY.
ONE IS CELSA GUTIERREZ, AN OLD FLAME.
ALTHOUGH NOW A MARRIED LADY, SHE AND THE KID HAVE RETAINED A STRONG BOND.
ANOTHER IS PAULITA MAXWELL, THE TEENAGE SISTER OF PETE MAXWELL, THE PRINCIPAL LANDOWNER IN FORT SUMNER.
RUMORS HAVE IT THAT SHE CARRIES THE OUTLAW'S CHILD.
SHELTER CAN BE FOUND AT THE OUTLYING SHEEP AND COW CAMPS OF FRIENDLY RANCHERS
FROM WHICH HE CAN VENTURE PERIODICALLY INTO TOWN.

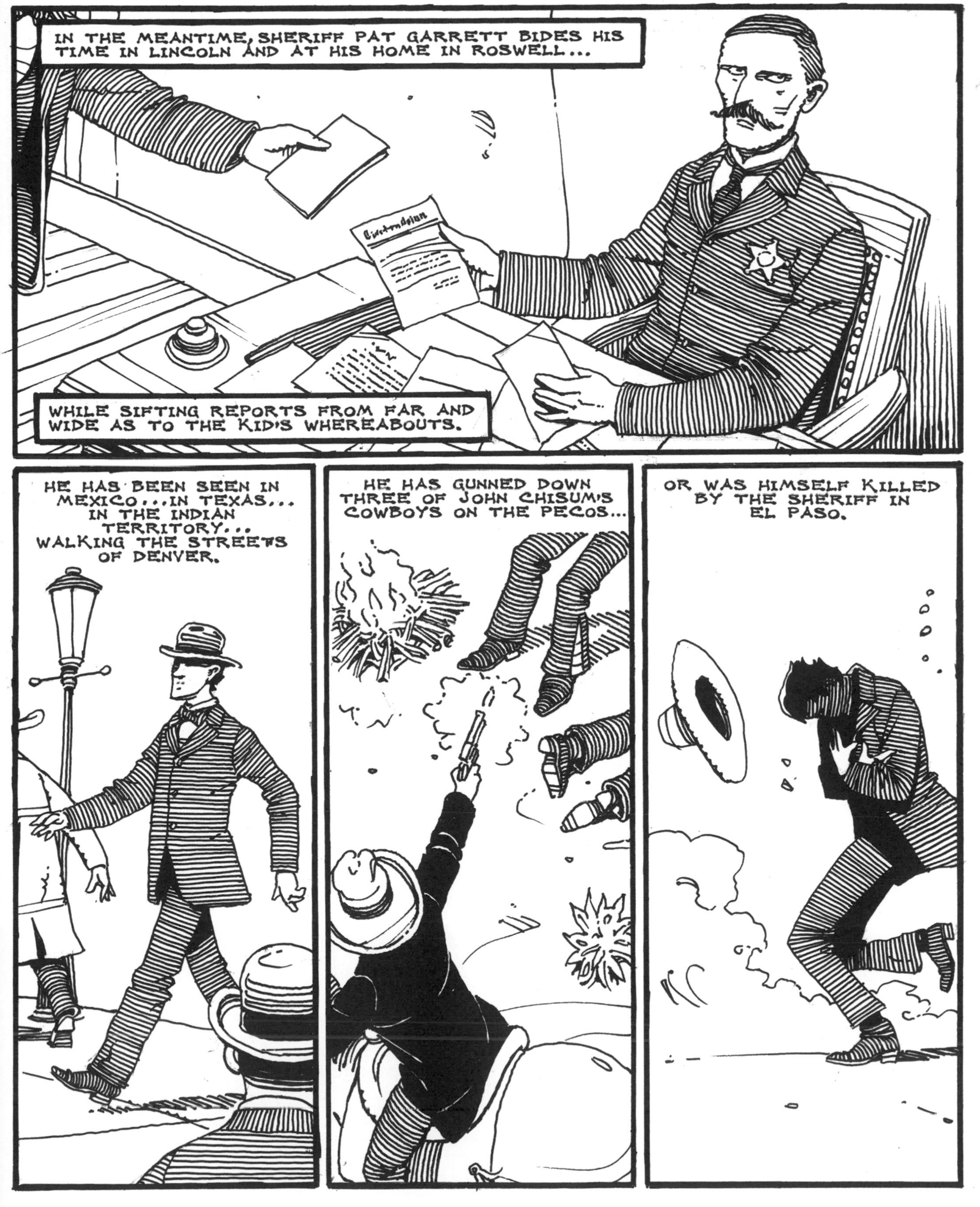
IN THE MEANTIME, SHERIFF PAT GARRETT BIDES HIS TIME IN LINCOLN AND AT HIS HOME IN ROSWELL...
WHILE SIFTING REPORTS FROM FAR AND WIDE AS TO THE KID'S WHEREABOUTS.
HE HAS BEEN SEEN IN MEXICO...IN TEXAS... IN THE INDIAN TERRITORY... WALKING THE STREETS OF DENVER.
HE HAS GUNNED DOWN THREE OF JOHN CHISUM'S COWBOYS ON THE PECOS...
OR WAS HIMSELF KILLED BY THE SHERIFF IN EL PASO.

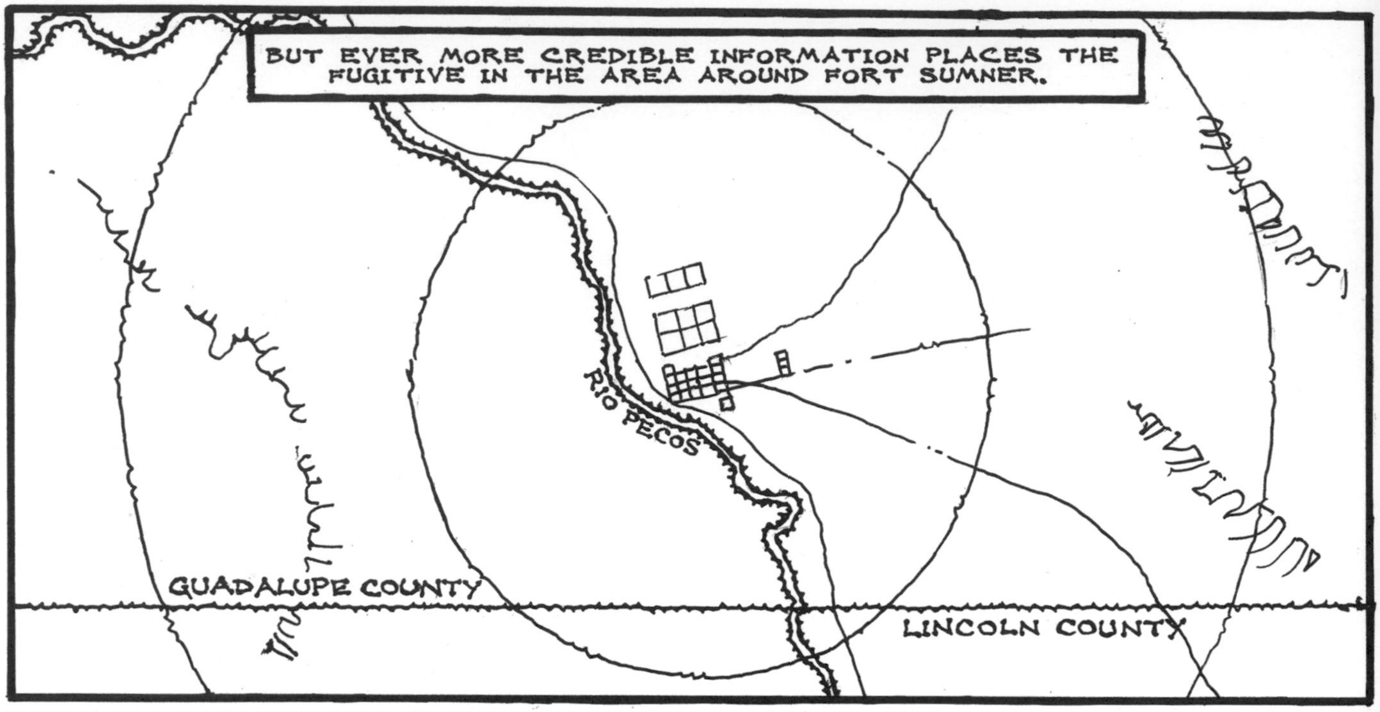
BUT EVER MORE CREDIBLE INFORMATION PLACES THE FUGITIVE IN THE AREA AROUND FORT SUMNER.
RIO PECOS
GUADALUPE COUNTY
LINCOLN COUNTY

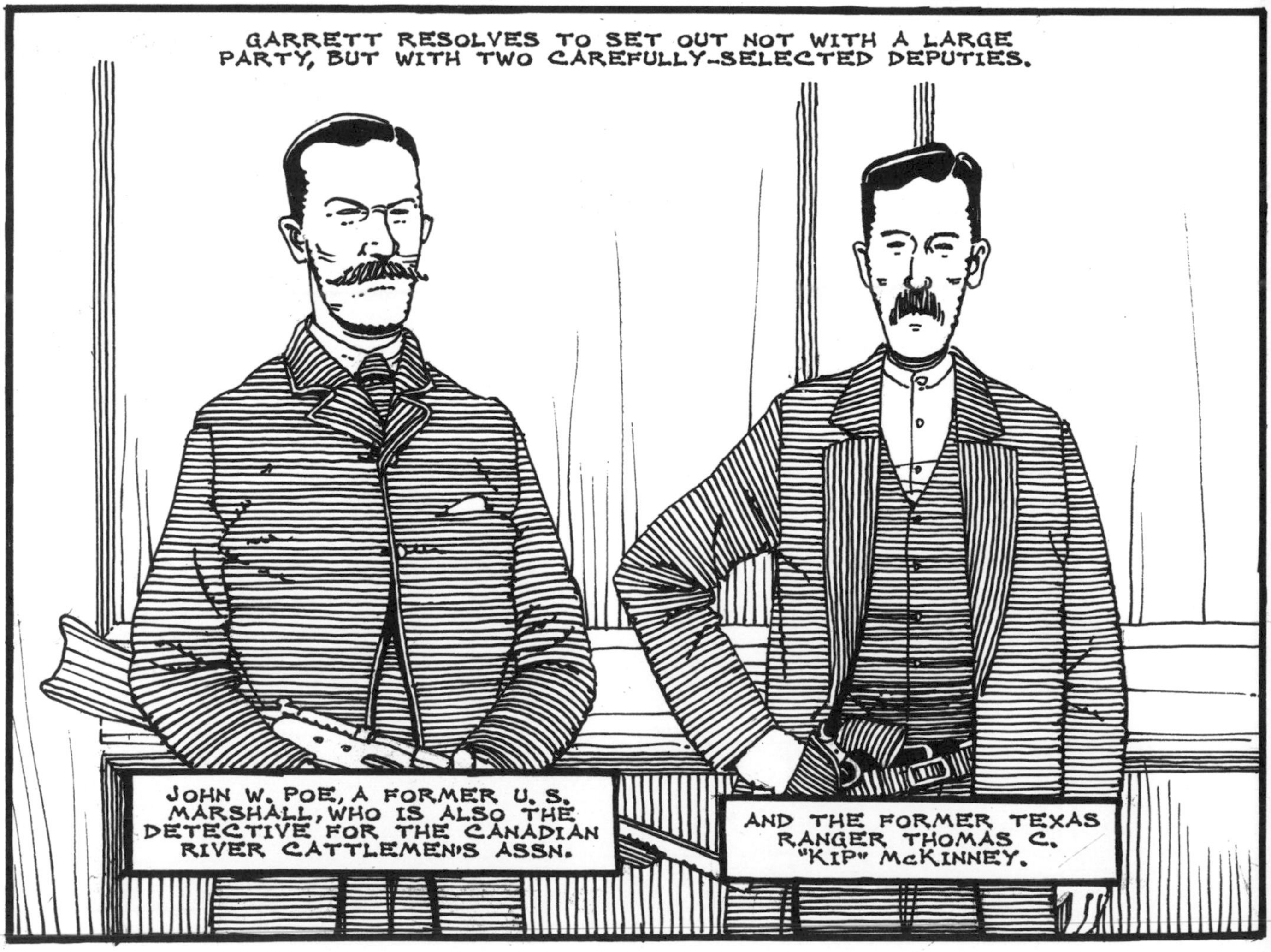
GARRETT RESOLVES TO SET OUT NOT WITH A LARGE PARTY, BUT WITH TWO CAREFULLY-SELECTED DEPUTIES.
JOHN W. POE, A FORMER U. S. MARSHALL, WHO IS ALSO THE DETECTIVE FOR THE CANADIAN RIVER CATTLEMEN'S ASSN.
AND THE FORMER TEXAS RANGER THOMAS C. "KIP" McKINNEY.

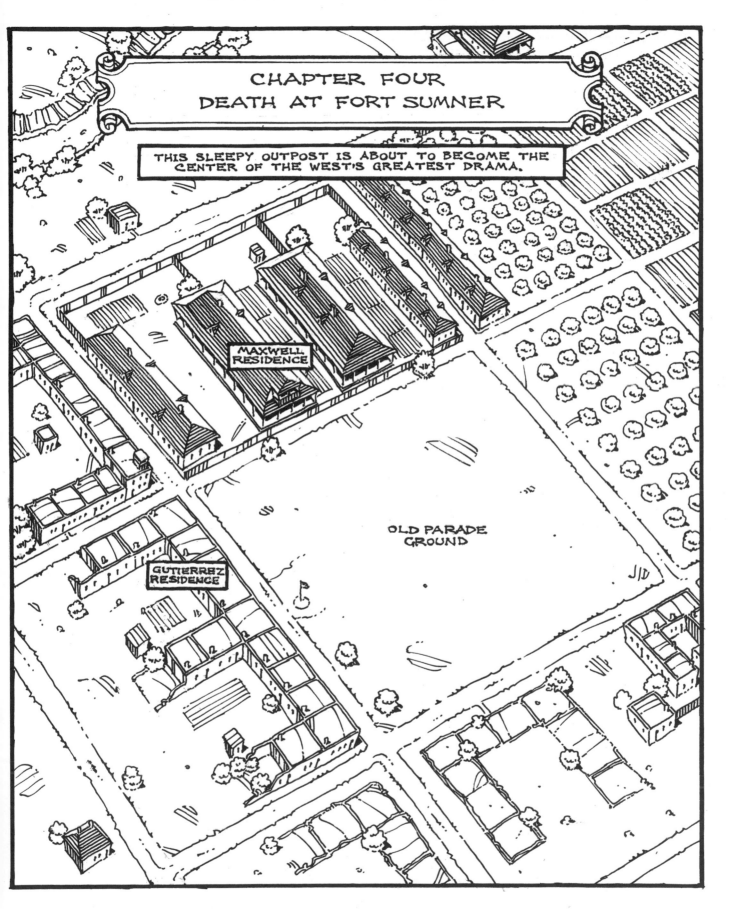

CHAPTER FOUR
DEATH AT FORT SUMNER

THIS SLEEPY OUTPOST IS ABOUT TO BECOME THE CENTER OF THE WEST'S GREATEST DRAMA.

MAXWELL RESIDENCE

GUTIERREZ RESIDENCE

OLD PARADE GROUND

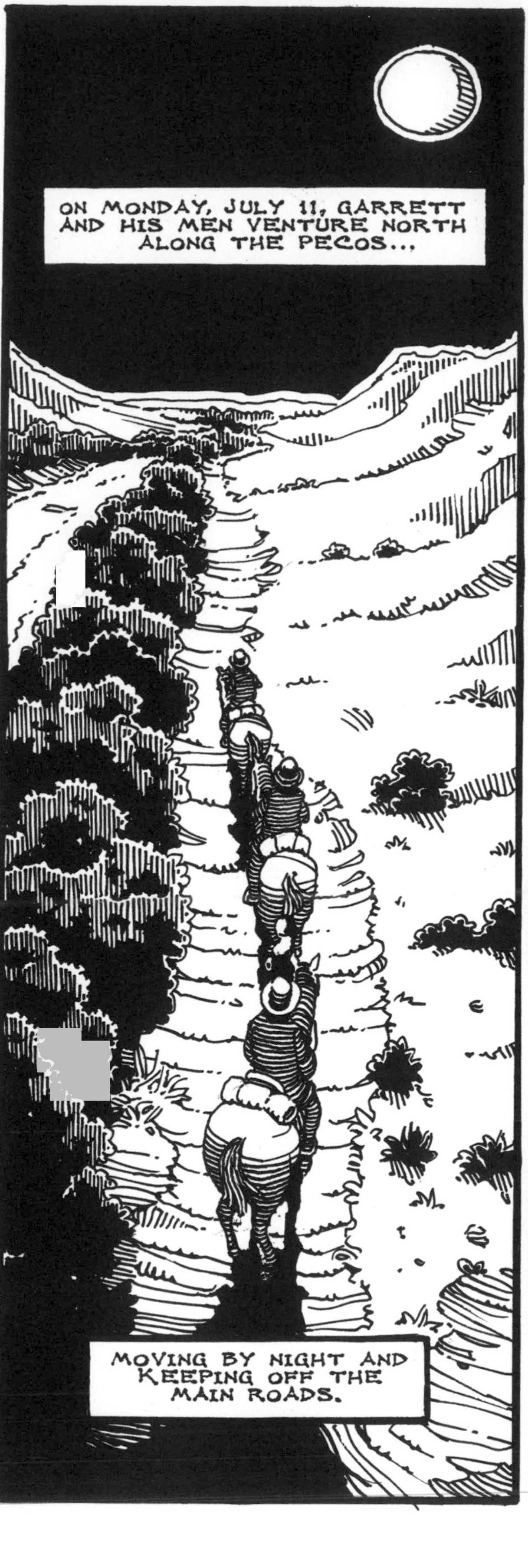
ON MONDAY, JULY 11, GARRETT AND HIS MEN VENTURE NORTH ALONG THE PECOS...
MOVING BY NIGHT AND KEEPING OFF THE MAIN ROADS.

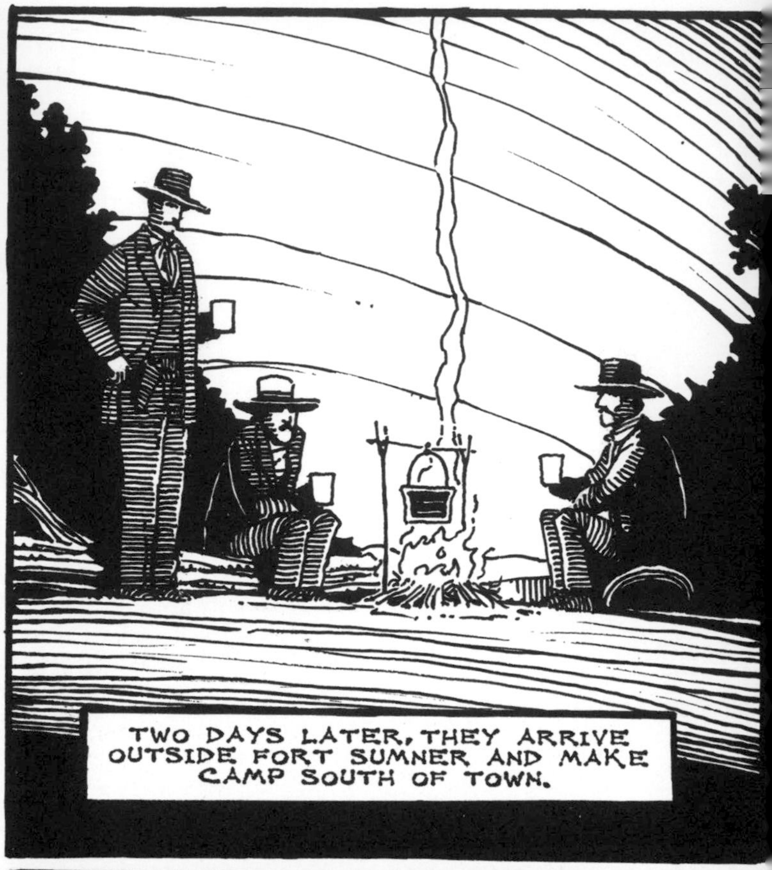
TWO DAYS LATER, THEY ARRIVE OUTSIDE FORT SUMNER AND MAKE CAMP SOUTH OF TOWN.

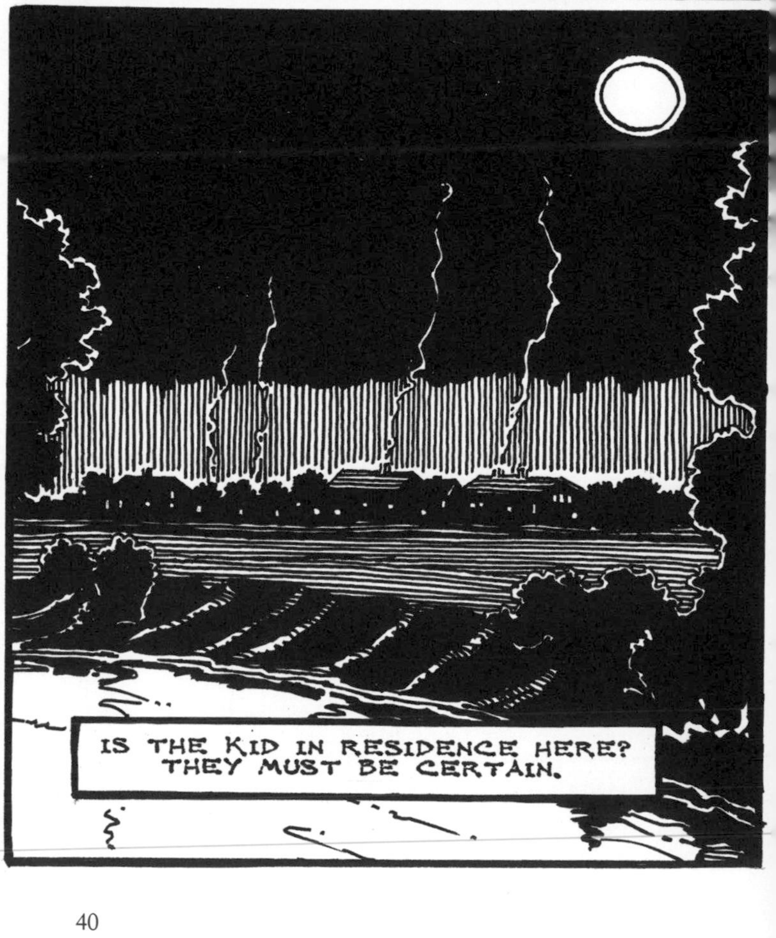
IS THE KID IN RESIDENCE HERE? THEY MUST BE CERTAIN.

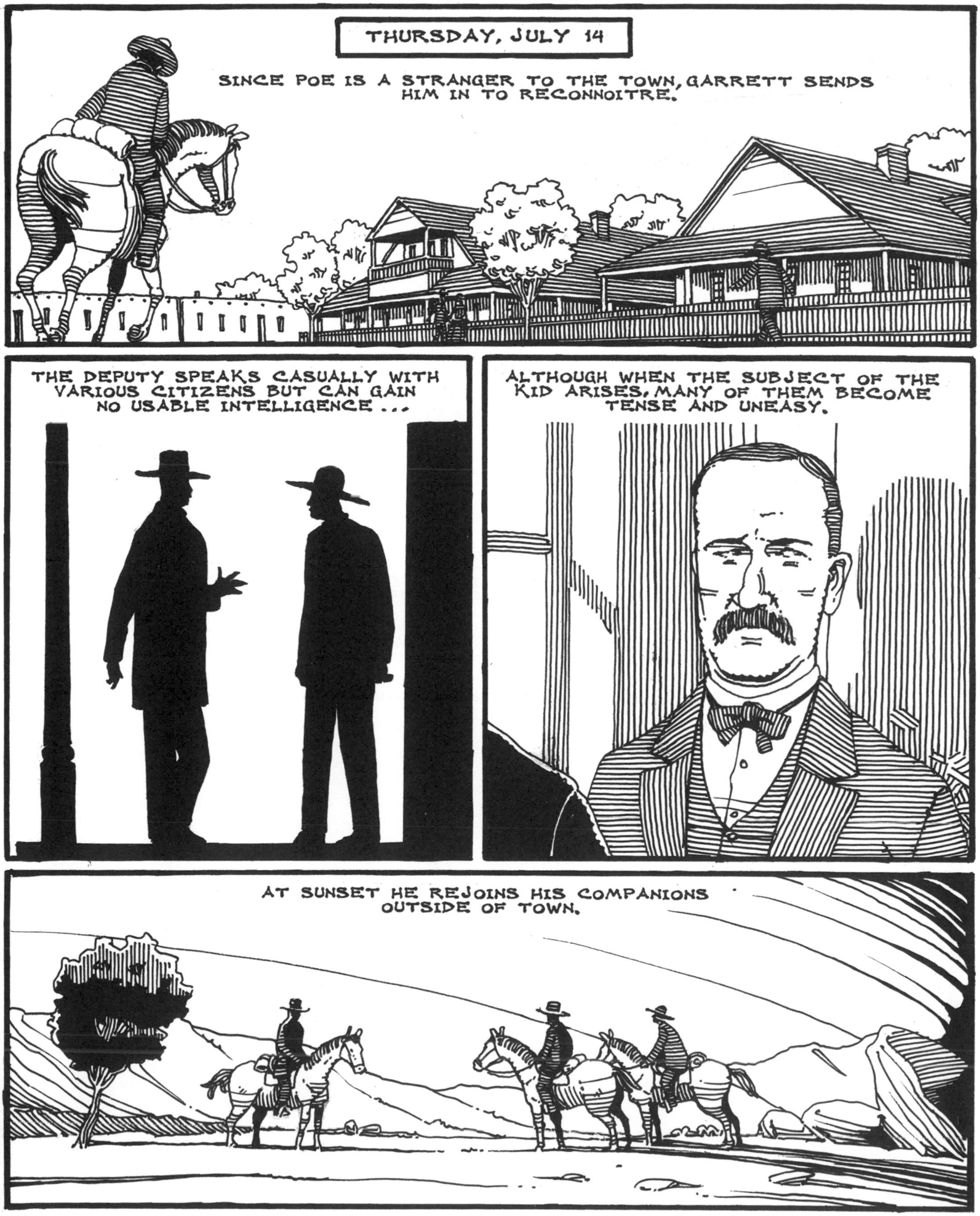
THURSDAY, JULY 14
SINCE POE IS A STRANGER TO THE TOWN, GARRETT SENDS HIM IN TO RECONNOITRE.
THE DEPUTY SPEAKS CASUALLY WITH VARIOUS CITIZENS BUT CAN GAIN NO USABLE INTELLIGENCE ...
ALTHOUGH WHEN THE SUBJECT OF THE KID ARISES, MANY OF THEM BECOME TENSE AND UNEASY.
AT SUNSET HE REJOINS HIS COMPANIONS OUTSIDE OF TOWN.

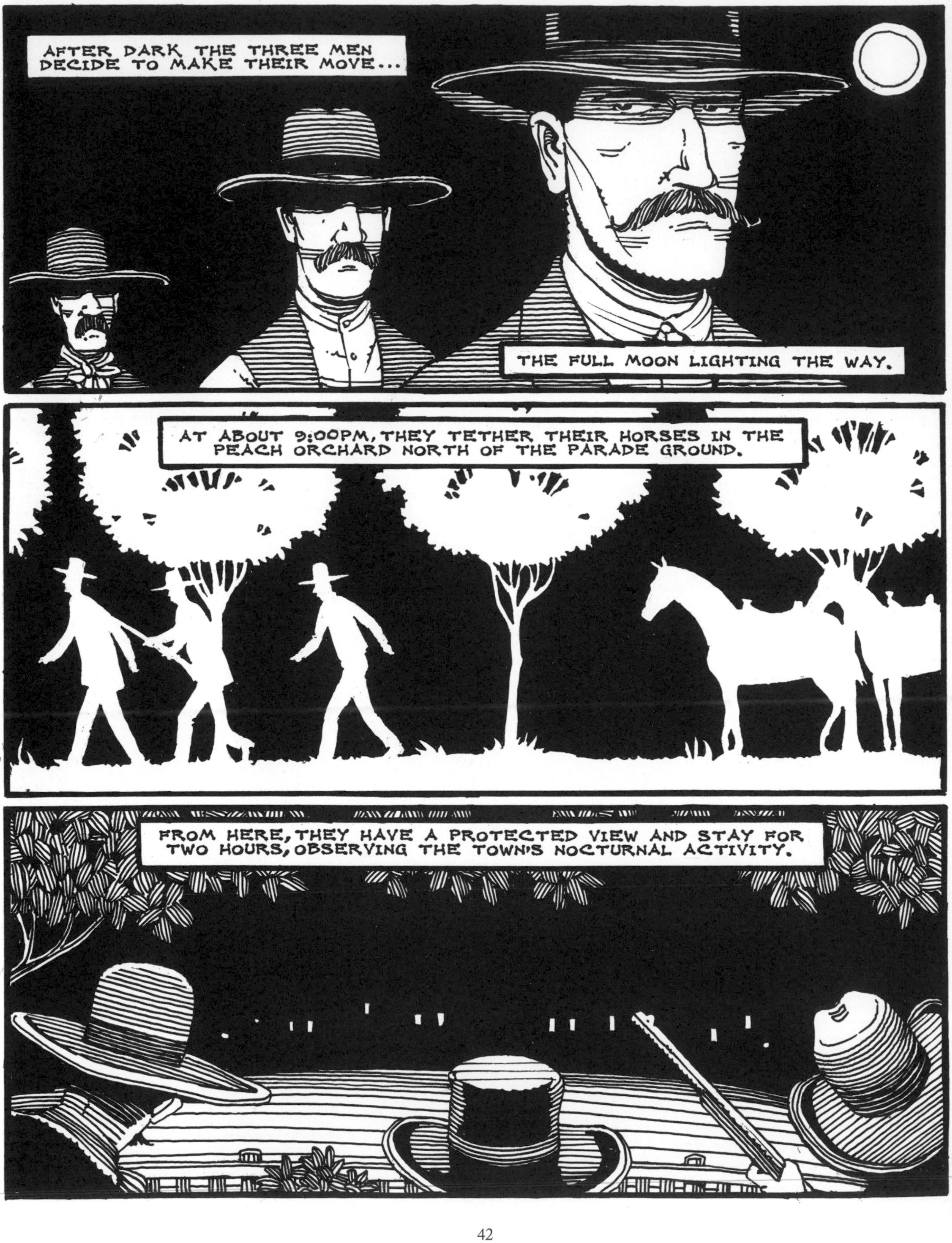
AFTER DARK THE THREE MEN DECIDE TO MAKE THEIR MOVE...
THE FULL MOON LIGHTING THE WAY.
AT ABOUT 9:00PM, THEY TETHER THEIR HORSES IN THE PEACH ORCHARD NORTH OF THE PARADE GROUND.
FROM HERE, THEY HAVE A PROTECTED VIEW AND STAY FOR TWO HOURS, OBSERVING THE TOWN'S NOCTURNAL ACTIVITY.

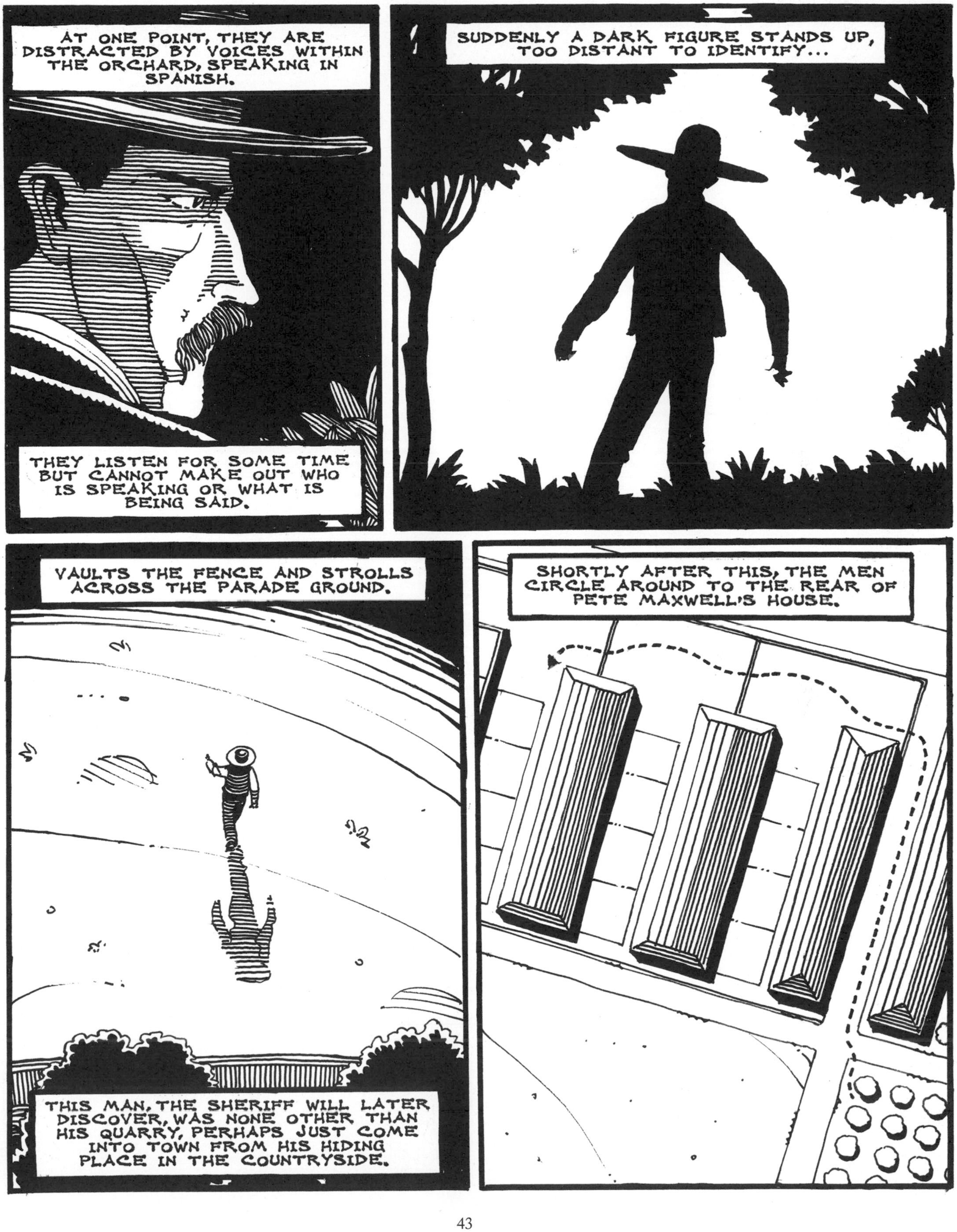
AT ONE POINT, THEY ARE DISTRACTED BY VOICES WITHIN THE ORCHARD, SPEAKING IN SPANISH.
THEY LISTEN FOR SOME TIME BUT CANNOT MAKE OUT WHO IS SPEAKING OR WHAT IS BEING SAID.
SUDDENLY A DARK FIGURE STANDS UP, TOO DISTANT TO IDENTIFY...
VAULTS THE FENCE AND STROLLS ACROSS THE PARADE GROUND.
THIS MAN, THE SHERIFF WILL LATER DISCOVER, WAS NONE OTHER THAN HIS QUARRY, PERHAPS JUST COME INTO TOWN FROM HIS HIDING PLACE IN THE COUNTRYSIDE.
SHORTLY AFTER THIS, THE MEN CIRCLE AROUND TO THE REAR OF PETE MAXWELL'S HOUSE.

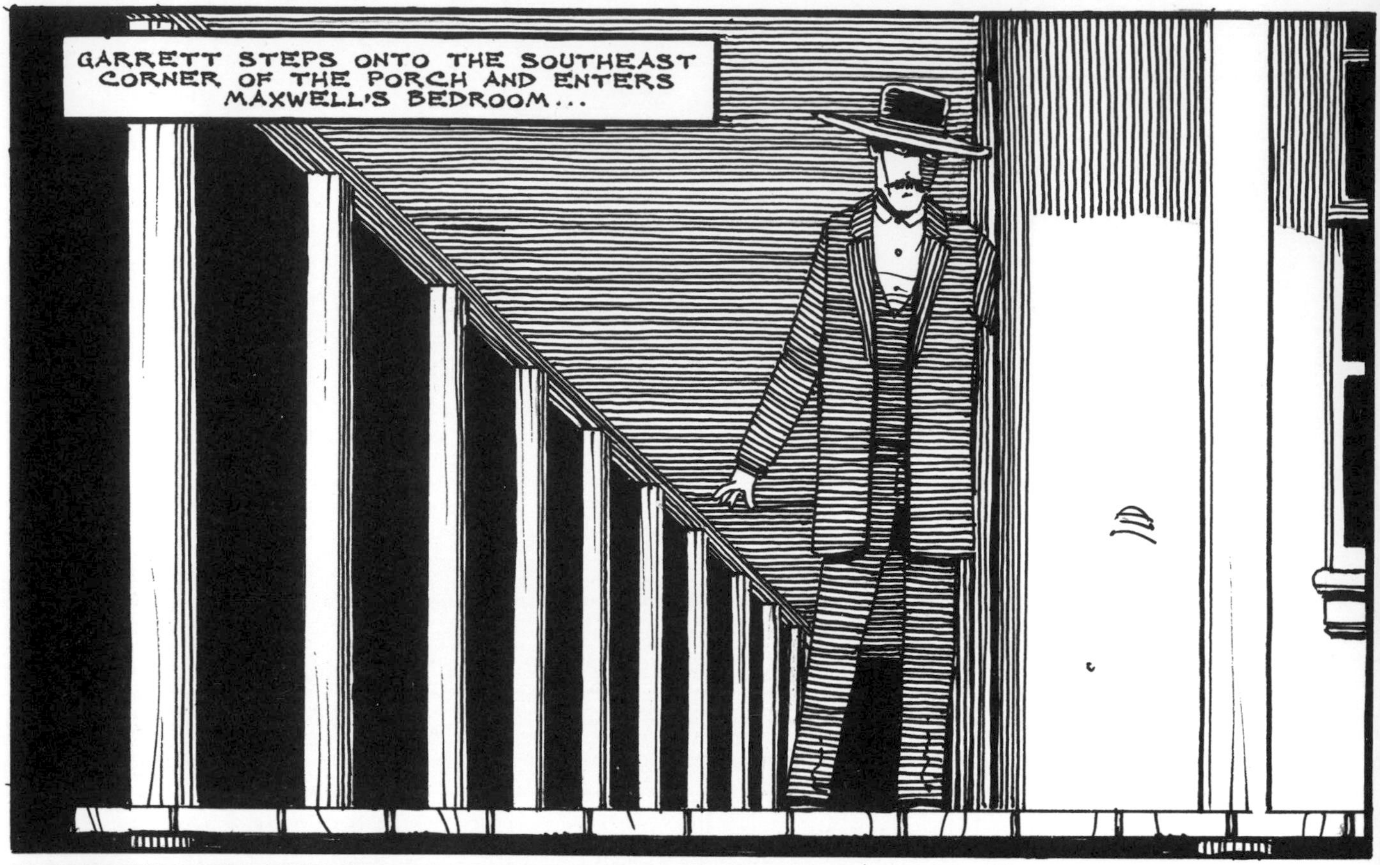
GARRETT STEPS ONTO THE SOUTHEAST CORNER OF THE PORCH AND ENTERS MAXWELL'S BEDROOM...

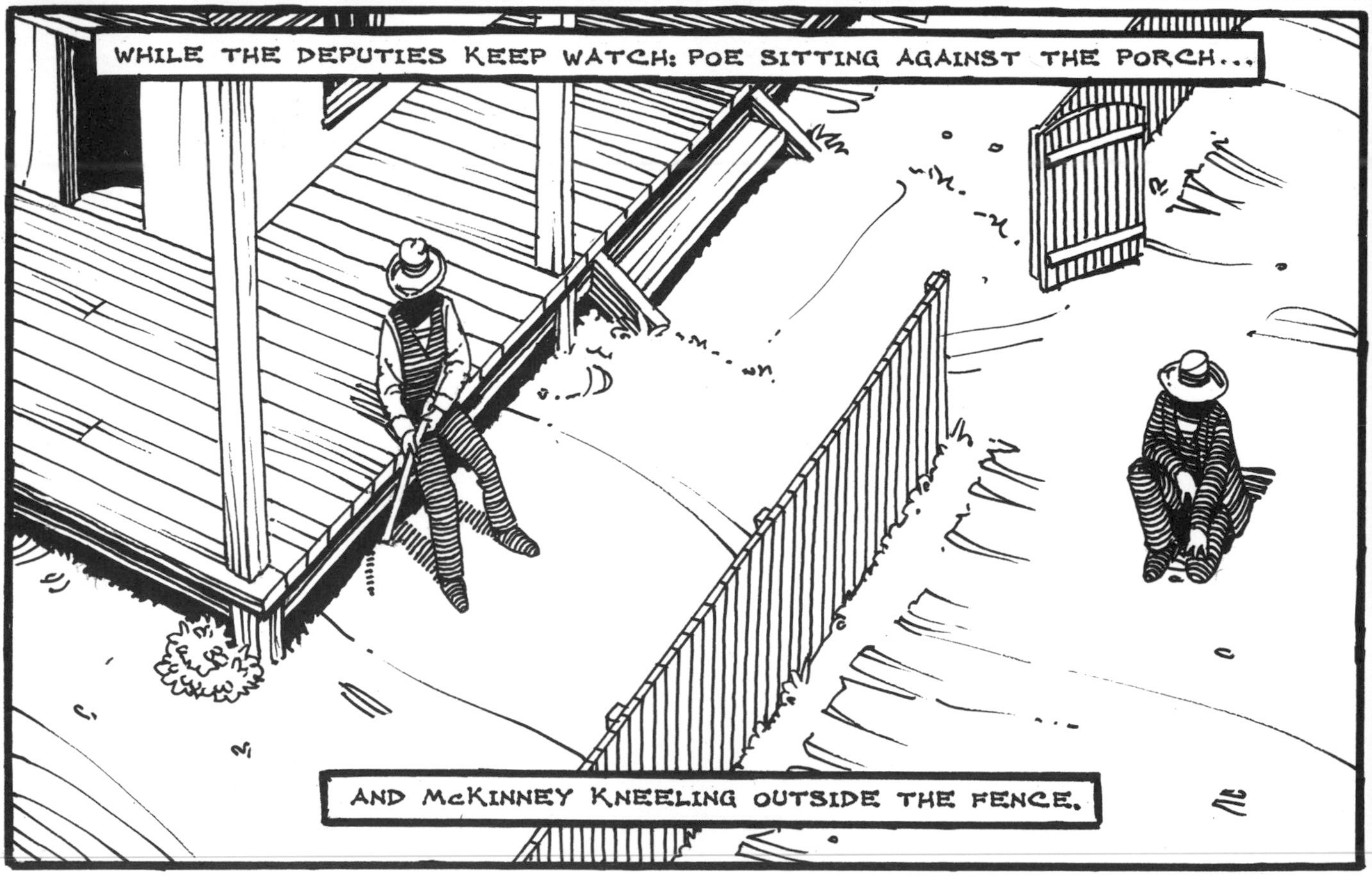
WHILE THE DEPUTIES KEEP WATCH: POE SITTING AGAINST THE PORCH...
AND McKINNEY KNEELING OUTSIDE THE FENCE.

WHERE IS THE KID AT THIS MOMENT?

BY SOME ACCOUNTS, HE IS RELAXING AT THE NEARBY RESIDENCE OF CELSA GUTIERREZ AND HER HUSBAND.

BUT HE COULD ALSO BE VISITING THE BEDROOM OF HIS CURRENT SWEETHEART PAULITA MAXWELL...

OR POSSIBLY THE HOME OF MANUELA BOWDRE, WIDOW OF HIS LATE FRIEND CHARLIE.

AT SOME POINT, HE VENTURES OUT INTO THE NIGHT.

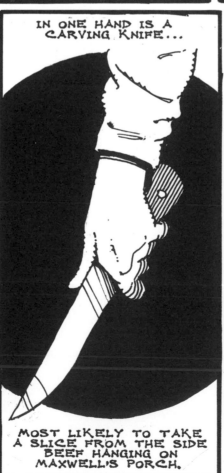

IN ONE HAND IS A CARVING KNIFE...

MOST LIKELY TO TAKE A SLICE FROM THE SIDE BEEF HANGING ON MAXWELL'S PORCH.

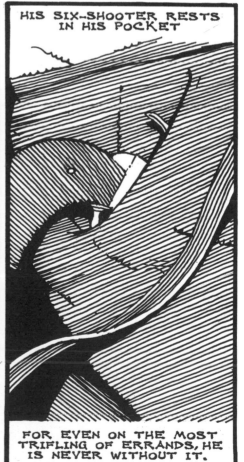

HIS SIX-SHOOTER RESTS IN HIS POCKET

FOR EVEN ON THE MOST TRIFLING OF ERRANDS, HE IS NEVER WITHOUT IT.

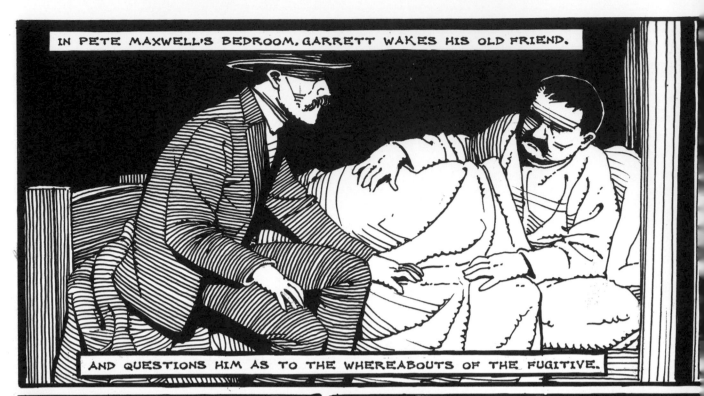

IN PETE MAXWELL'S BEDROOM, GARRETT WAKES HIS OLD FRIEND.

AND QUESTIONS HIM AS TO THE WHEREABOUTS OF THE FUGITIVE.

MAXWELL, THOUGH, SEEMS UNCOMFORTABLE AND IS UNWILLING TO GIVE UP ANY INFORMATION.

THE TWO HEAR VOICES FROM OUTSIDE.

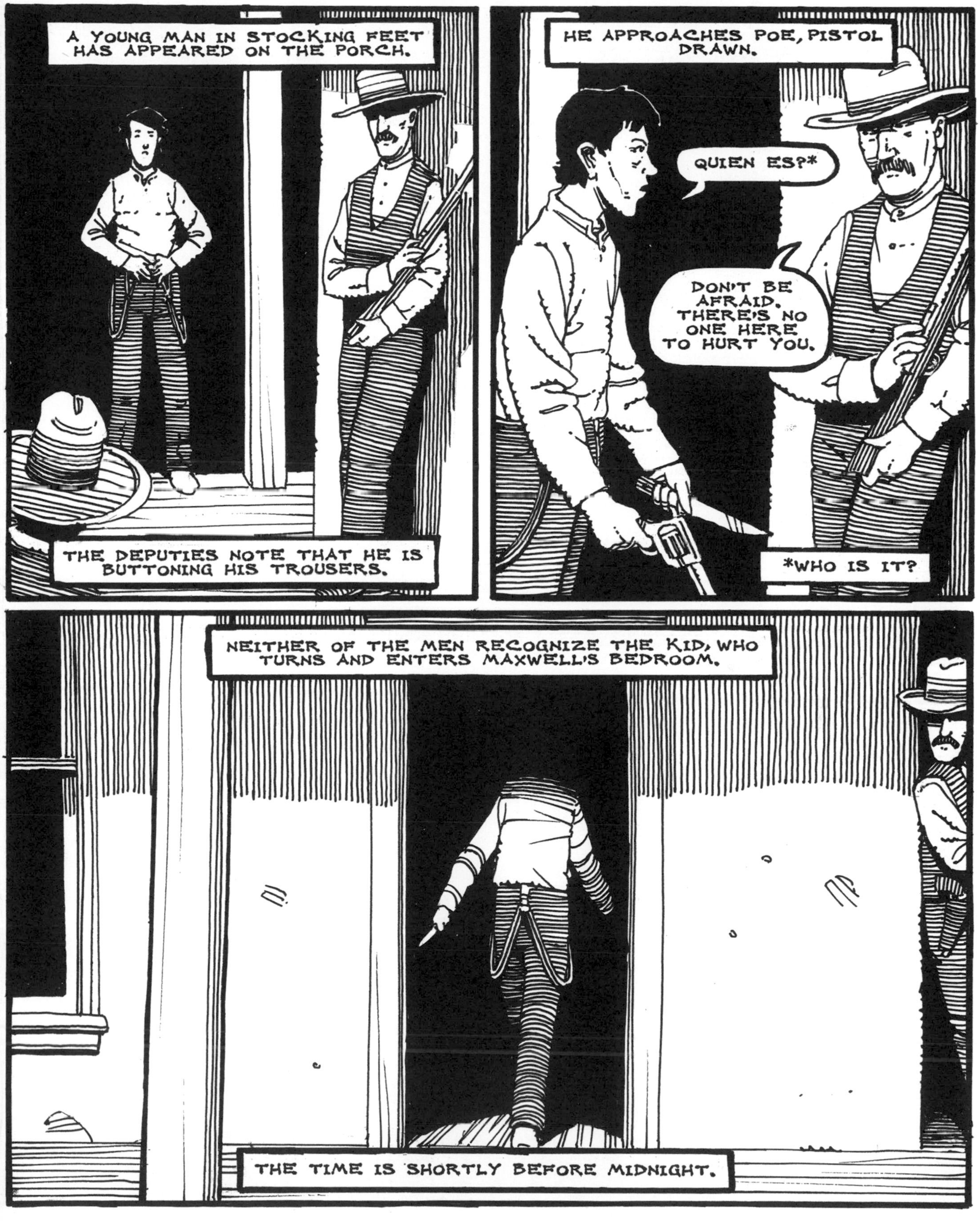
A YOUNG MAN IN STOCKING FEET HAS APPEARED ON THE PORCH.
THE DEPUTIES NOTE THAT HE IS BUTTONING HIS TROUSERS.
HE APPROACHES POE, PISTOL DRAWN.
QUIEN ES?*
DON'T BE AFRAID. THERE'S NO ONE HERE TO HURT YOU.
*WHO IS IT?
NEITHER OF THE MEN RECOGNIZE THE KID, WHO TURNS AND ENTERS MAXWELL'S BEDROOM.
THE TIME IS SHORTLY BEFORE MIDNIGHT.

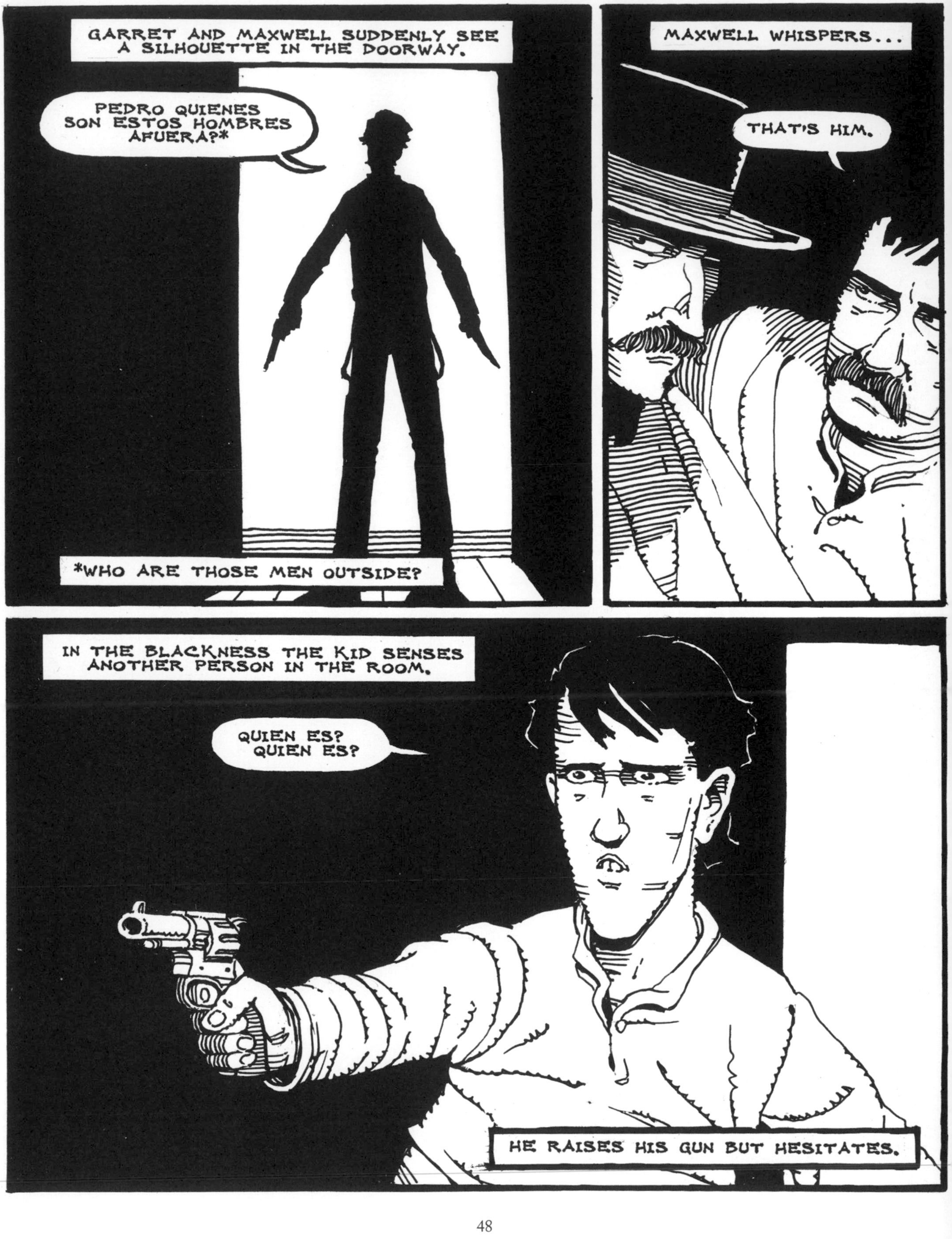
GARRET AND MAXWELL SUDDENLY SEE A SILHOUETTE IN THE DOORWAY.
PEDRO QUIENES SON ESTOS HOMBRES AFUERA?*
*WHO ARE THOSE MEN OUTSIDE?
MAXWELL WHISPERS...
THAT'S HIM.
IN THE BLACKNESS THE KID SENSES ANOTHER PERSON IN THE ROOM.
QUIEN ES? QUIEN ES?
HE RAISES HIS GUN BUT HESITATES.

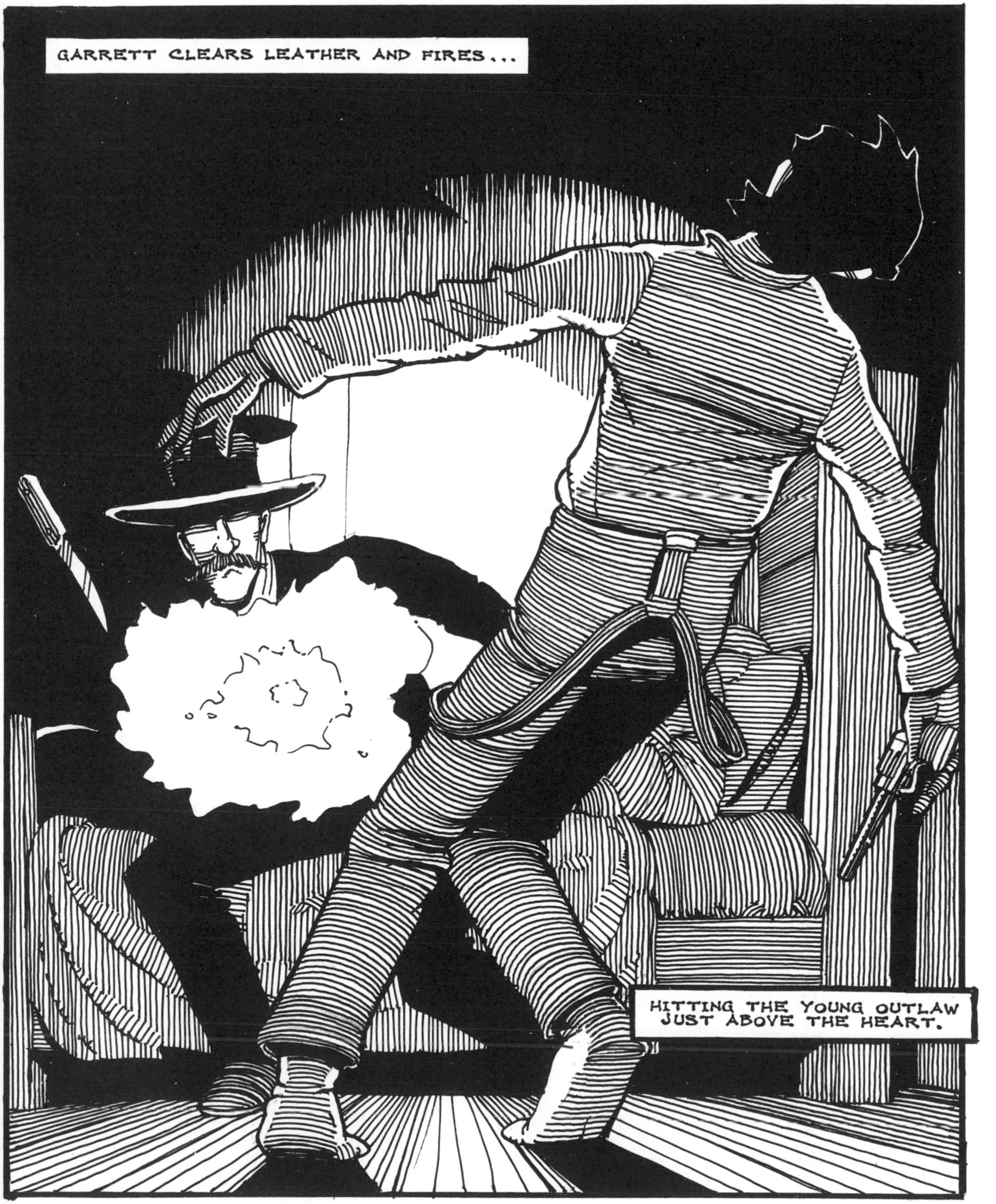
GARRETT CLEARS LEATHER AND FIRES...
HITTING THE YOUNG OUTLAW JUST ABOVE THE HEART.

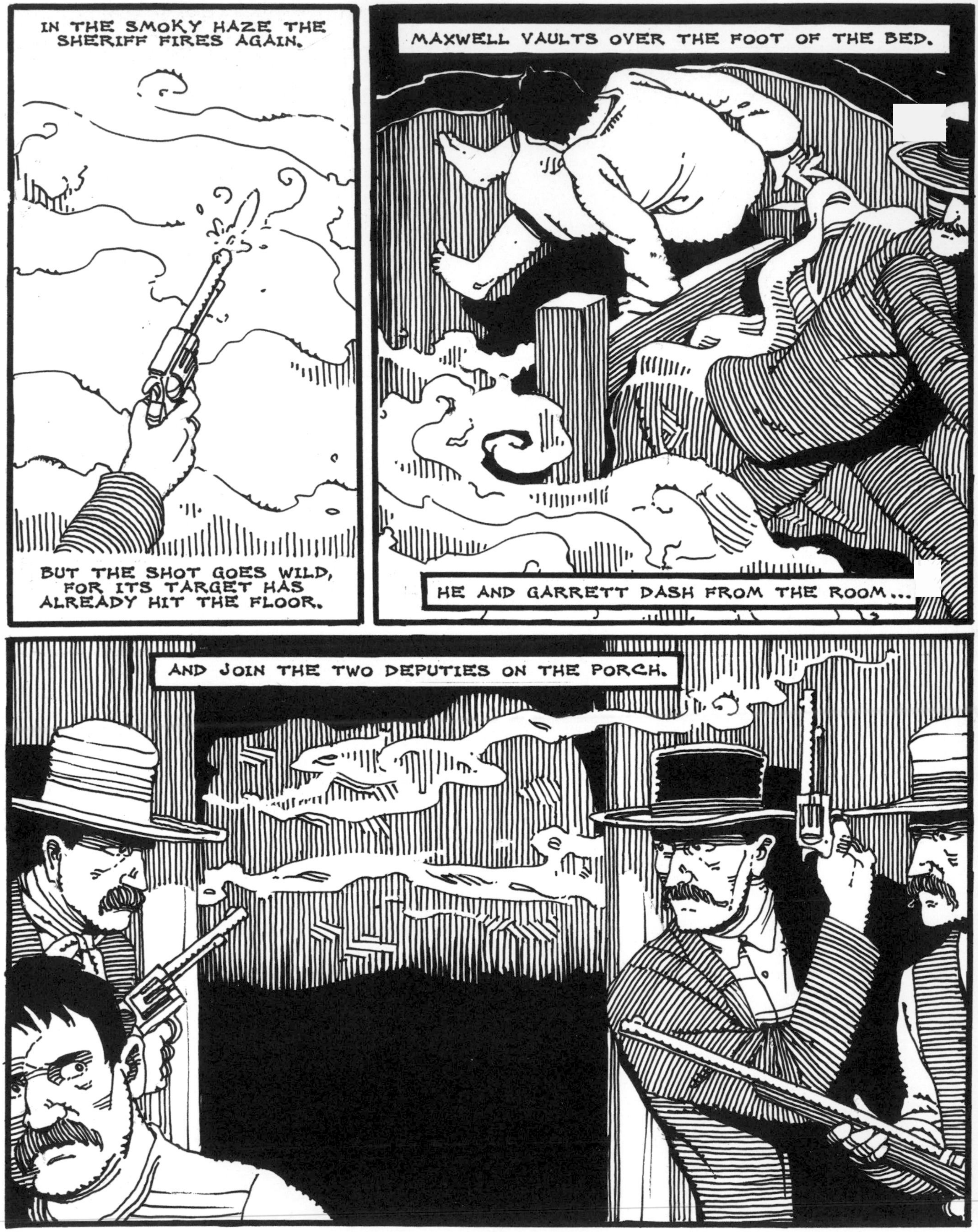
IN THE SMOKY HAZE THE SHERIFF FIRES AGAIN.
BUT THE SHOT GOES WILD, FOR ITS TARGET HAS ALREADY HIT THE FLOOR.
MAXWELL VAULTS OVER THE FOOT OF THE BED.
HE AND GARRETT DASH FROM THE ROOM...
AND JOIN THE TWO DEPUTIES ON THE PORCH.

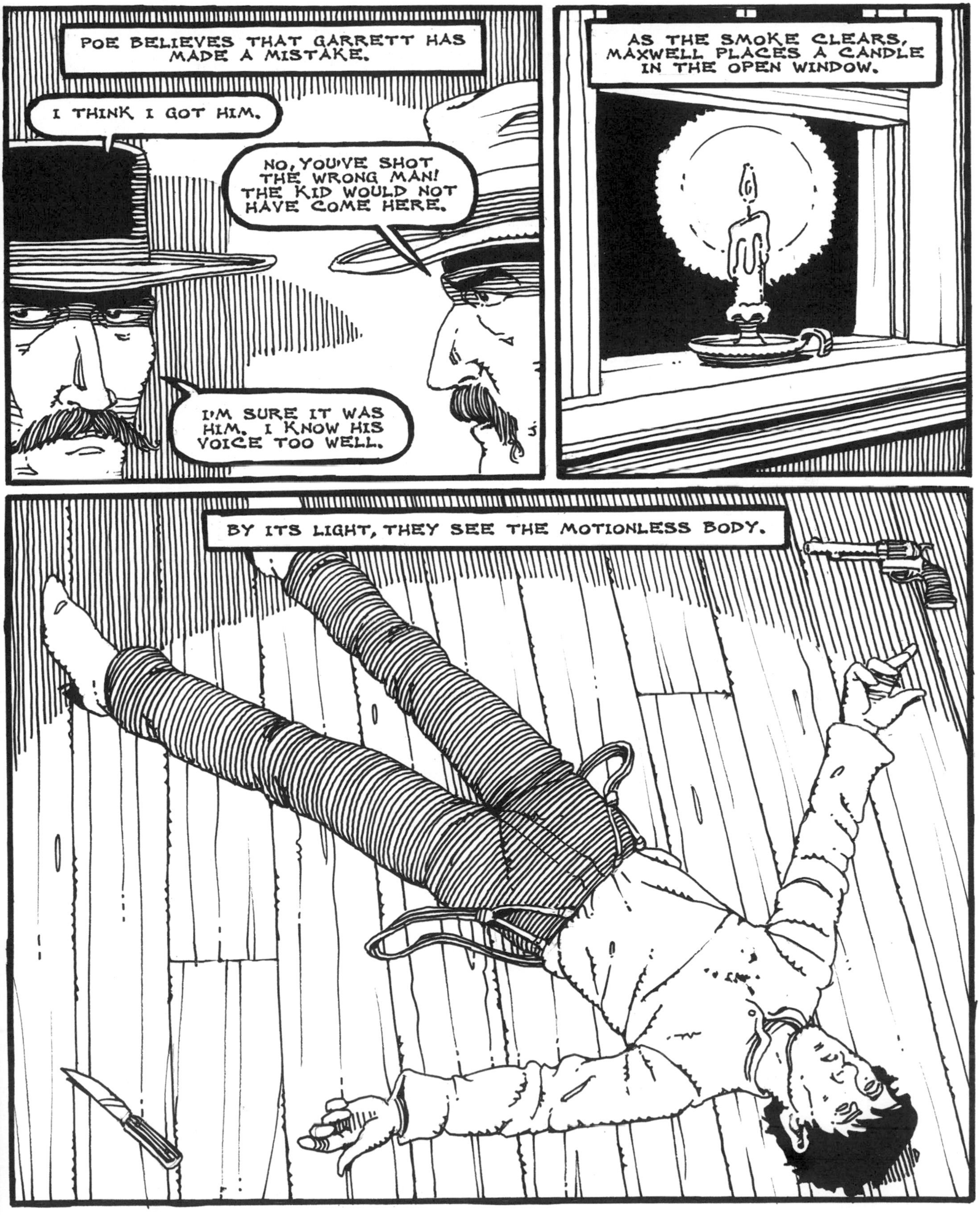
POE BELIEVES THAT GARRETT HAS MADE A MISTAKE.
I THINK I GOT HIM.
NO, YOU'VE SHOT THE WRONG MAN! THE KID WOULD NOT HAVE COME HERE.
I'M SURE IT WAS HIM. I KNOW HIS VOICE TOO WELL.
AS THE SMOKE CLEARS, MAXWELL PLACES A CANDLE IN THE OPEN WINDOW.
BY ITS LIGHT, THEY SEE THE MOTIONLESS BODY.

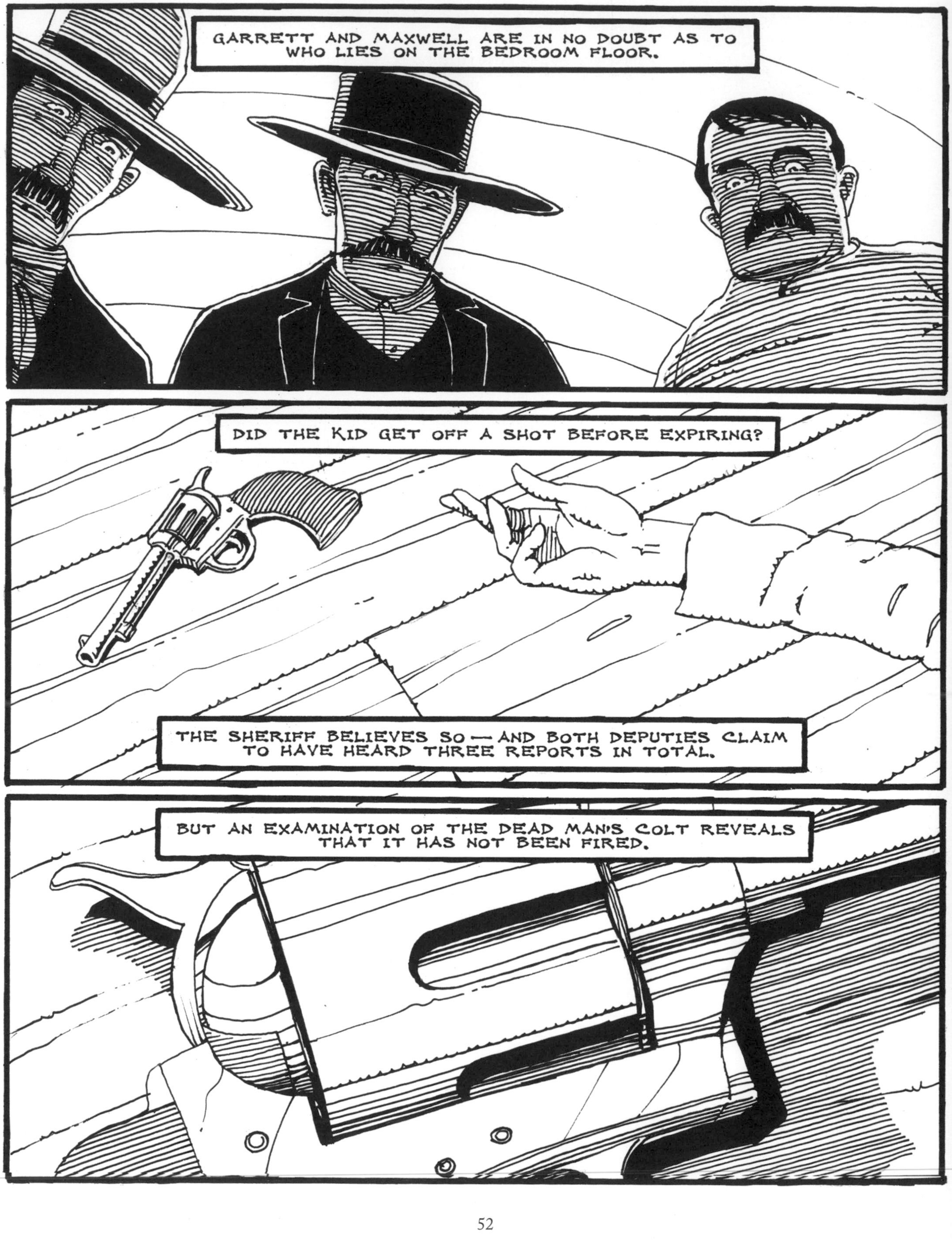
GARRETT AND MAXWELL ARE IN NO DOUBT AS TO WHO LIES ON THE BEDROOM FLOOR.
DID THE KID GET OFF A SHOT BEFORE EXPIRING?
THE SHERIFF BELIEVES SO — AND BOTH DEPUTIES CLAIM TO HAVE HEARD THREE REPORTS IN TOTAL.
BUT AN EXAMINATION OF THE DEAD MAN'S COLT REVEALS THAT IT HAS NOT BEEN FIRED.

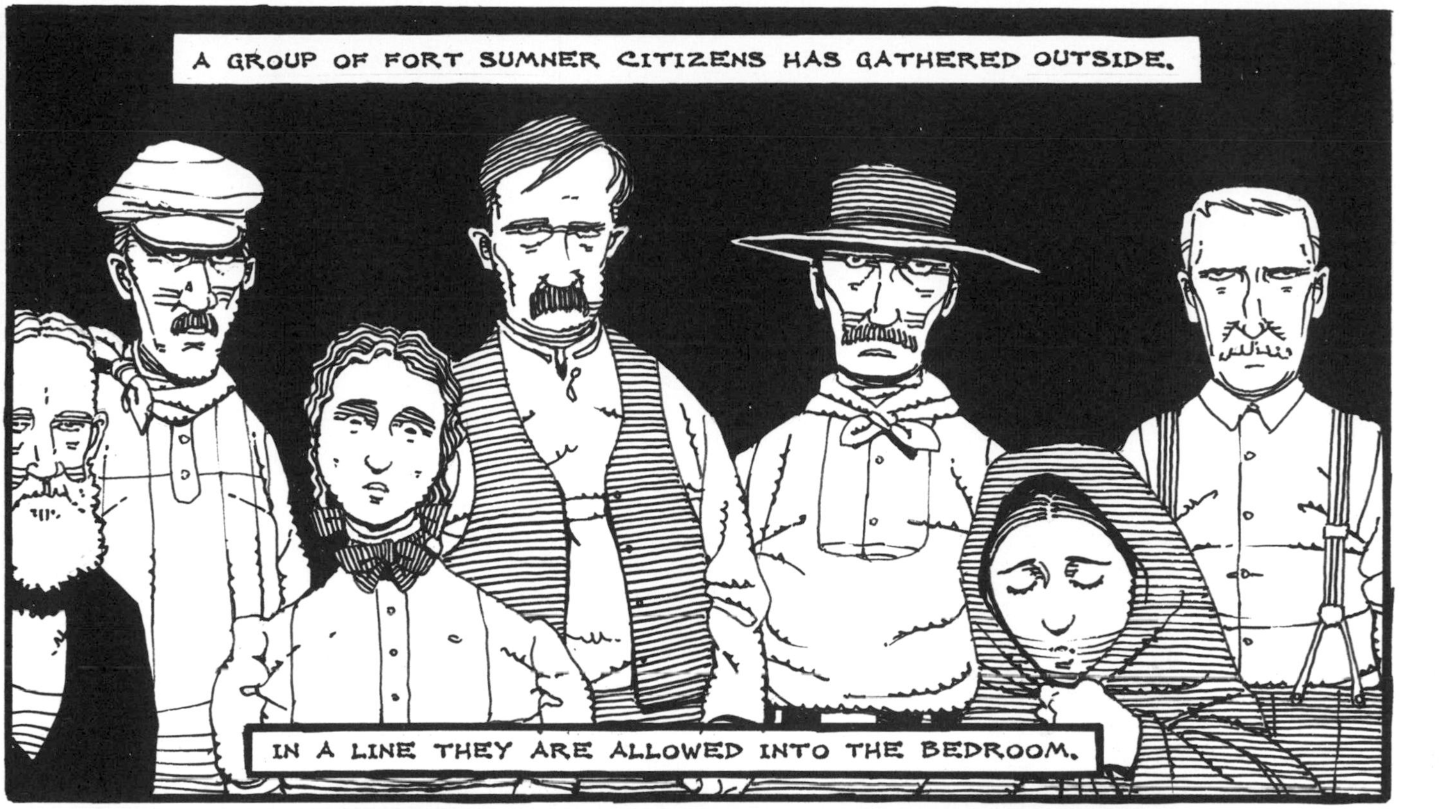
A GROUP OF FORT SUMNER CITIZENS HAS GATHERED OUTSIDE.
IN A LINE THEY ARE ALLOWED INTO THE BEDROOM.

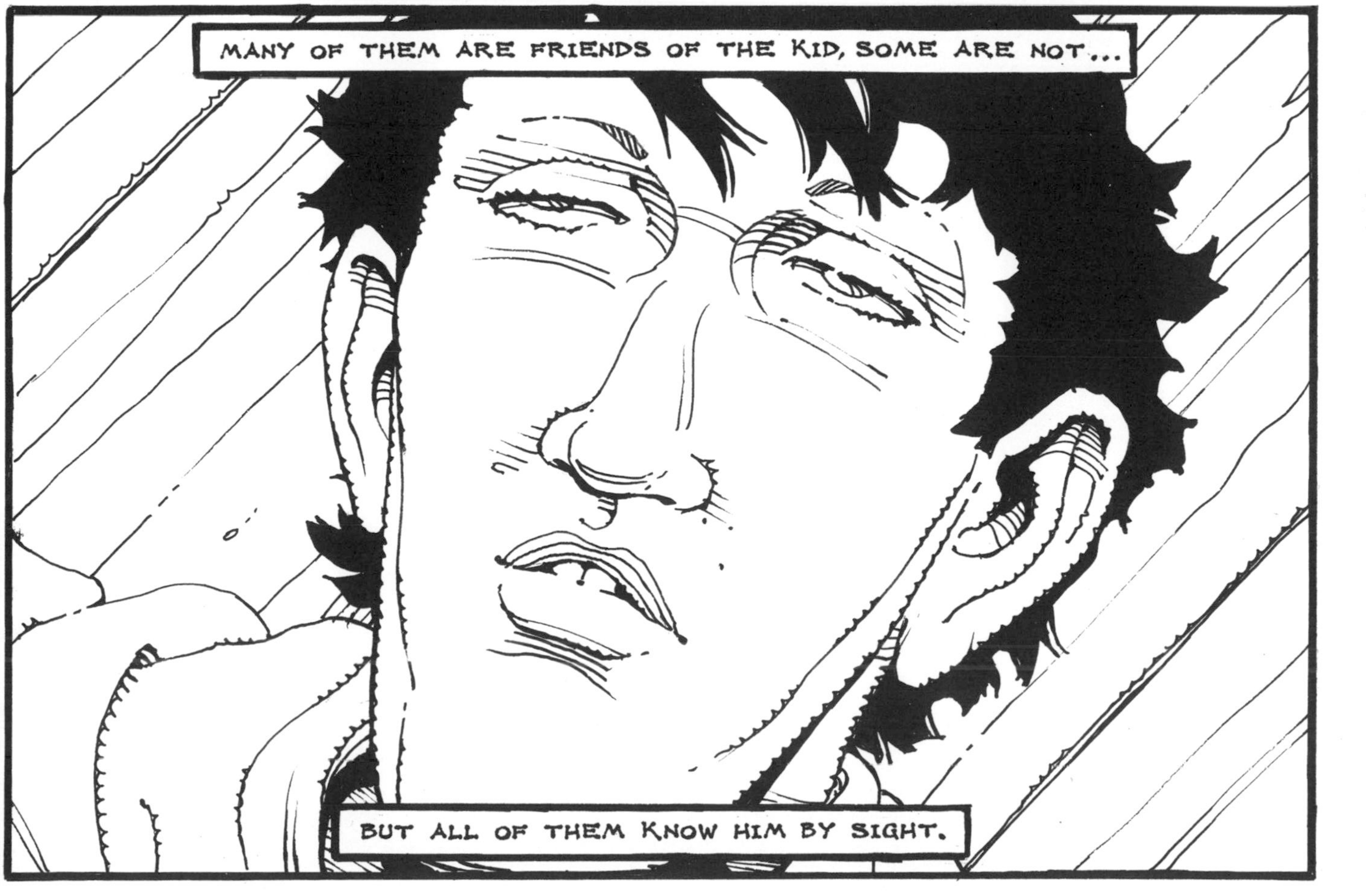
MANY OF THEM ARE FRIENDS OF THE KID, SOME ARE NOT...
BUT ALL OF THEM KNOW HIM BY SIGHT.

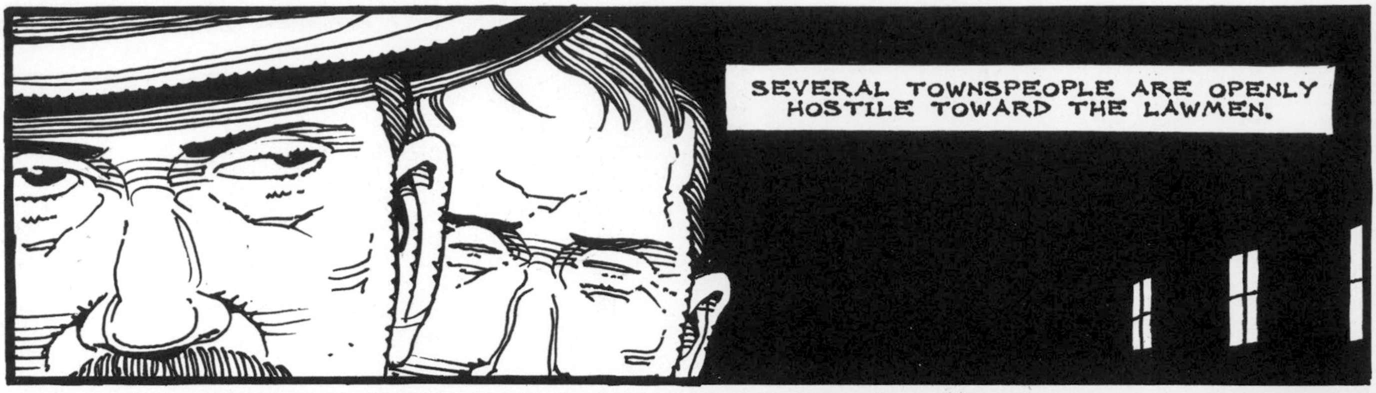
SEVERAL TOWNSPEOPLE ARE OPENLY HOSTILE TOWARD THE LAWMEN.

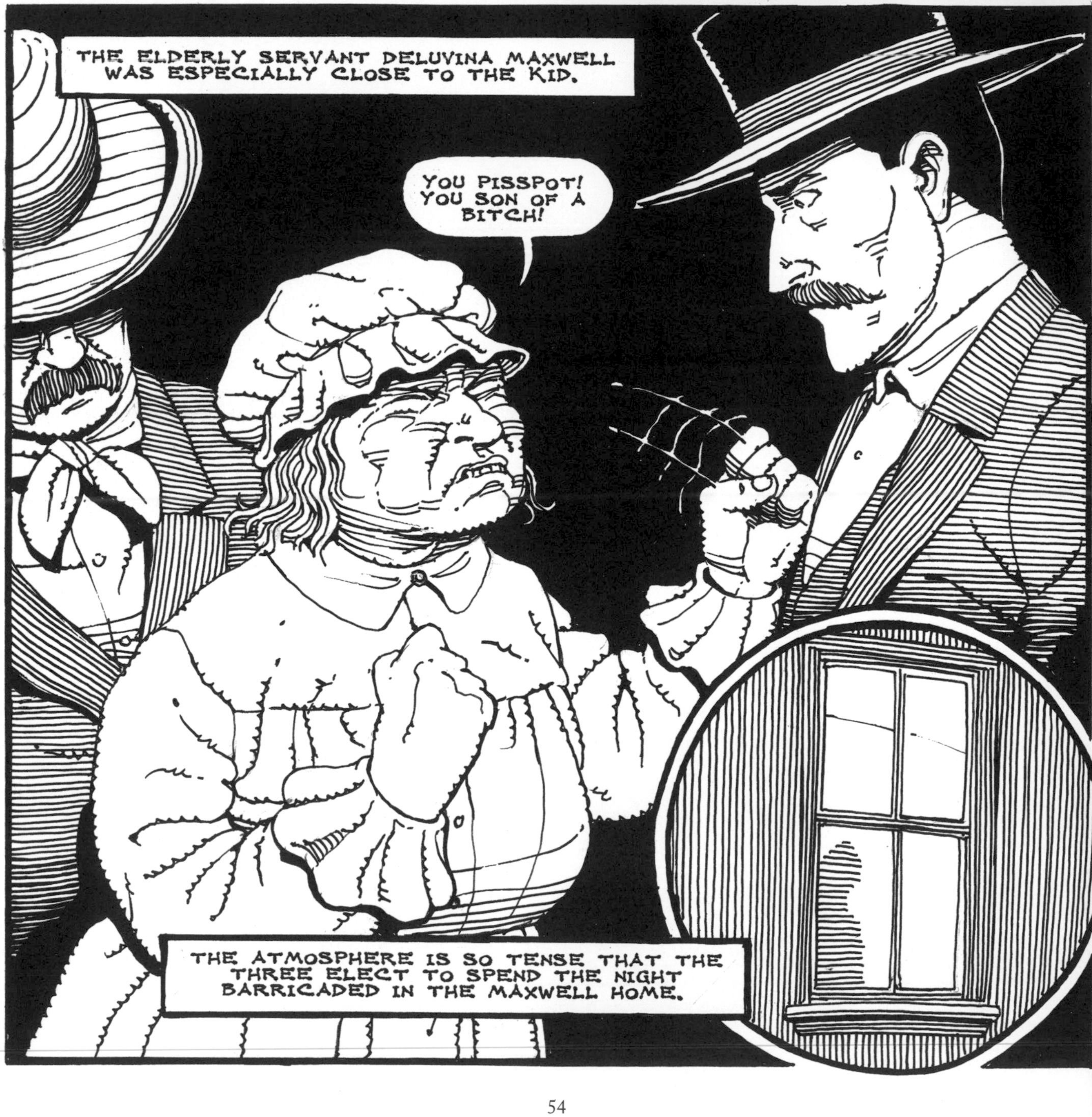
THE ELDERLY SERVANT DELUVINA MAXWELL WAS ESPECIALLY CLOSE TO THE KID.
YOU PISSPOT! YOU SON OF A BITCH!
THE ATMOSPHERE IS SO TENSE THAT THE THREE ELECT TO SPEND THE NIGHT BARRICADED IN THE MAXWELL HOME.

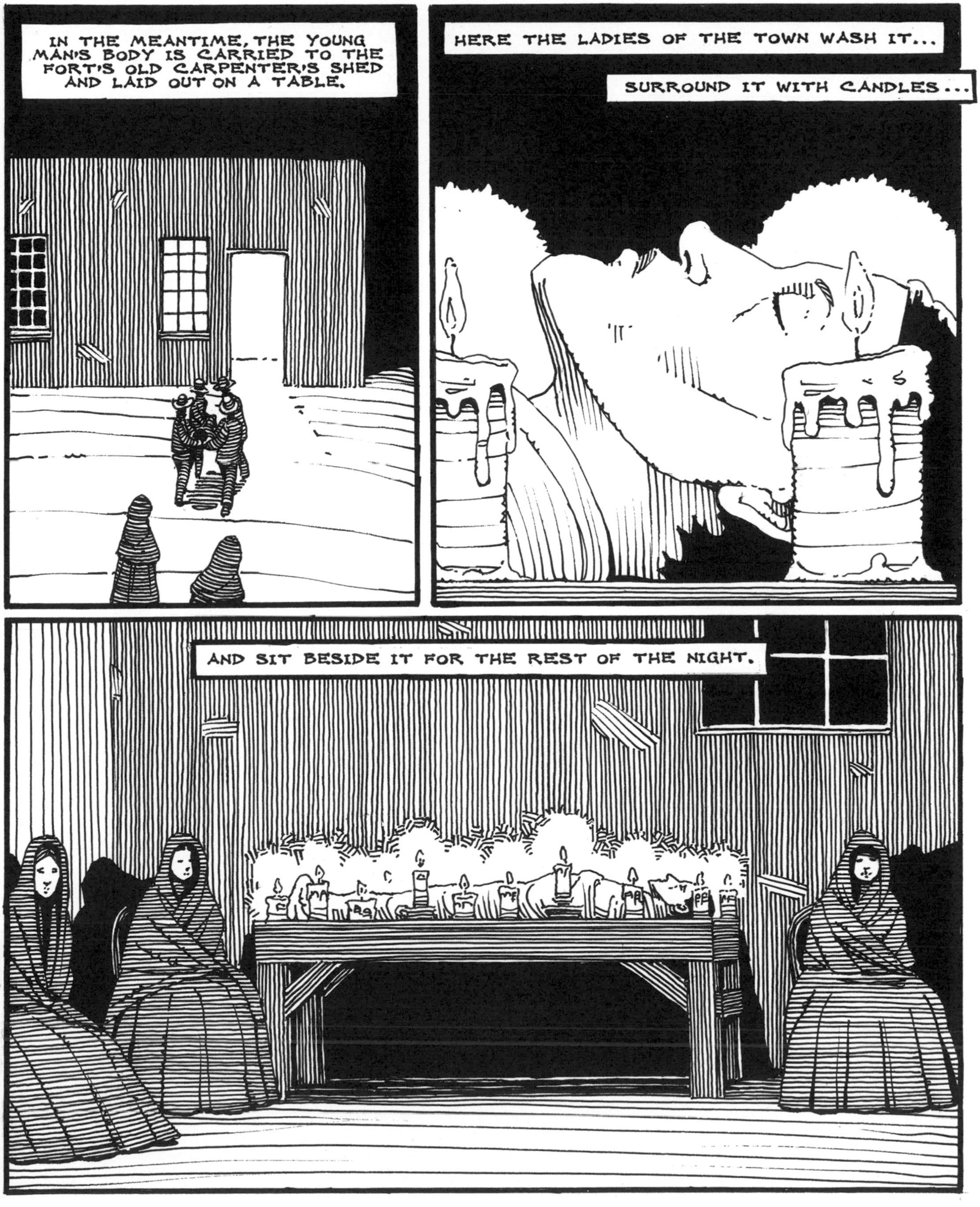
IN THE MEANTIME, THE YOUNG MAN'S BODY IS CARRIED TO THE FORT'S OLD CARPENTER'S SHED AND LAID OUT ON A TABLE.
HERE THE LADIES OF THE TOWN WASH IT...
SURROUND IT WITH CANDLES...
AND SIT BESIDE IT FOR THE REST OF THE NIGHT.

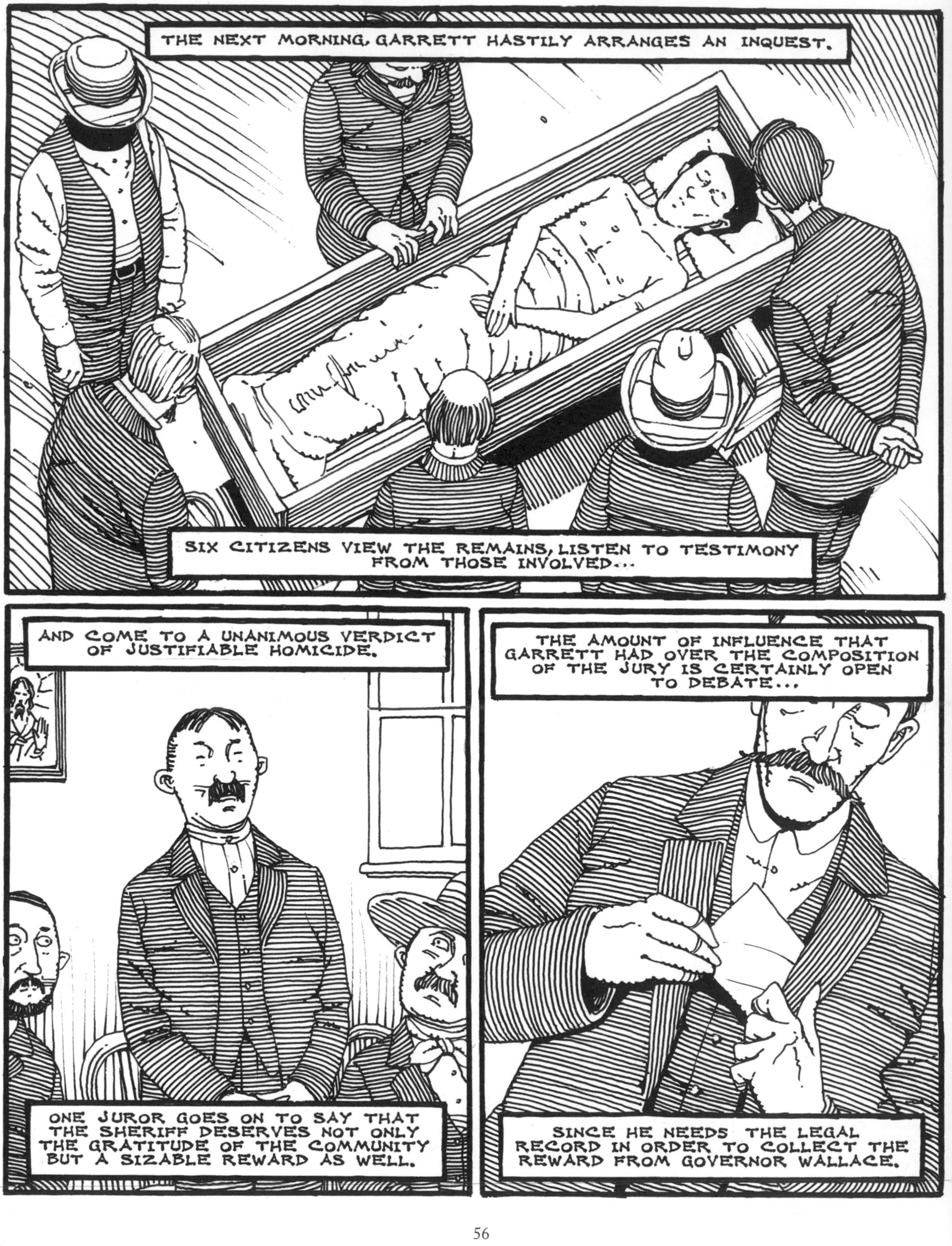
THE NEXT MORNING, GARRETT HASTILY ARRANGES AN INQUEST.
SIX CITIZENS VIEW THE REMAINS, LISTEN TO TESTIMONY FROM THOSE INVOLVED...
AND COME TO A UNANIMOUS VERDICT OF JUSTIFIABLE HOMICIDE.
ONE JUROR GOES ON TO SAY THAT THE SHERIFF DESERVES NOT ONLY THE GRATITUDE OF THE COMMUNITY BUT A SIZABLE REWARD AS WELL.
THE AMOUNT OF INFLUENCE THAT GARRETT HAD OVER THE COMPOSITION OF THE JURY IS CERTAINLY OPEN TO DEBATE...
SINCE HE NEEDS THE LEGAL RECORD IN ORDER TO COLLECT THE REWARD FROM GOVERNOR WALLACE.

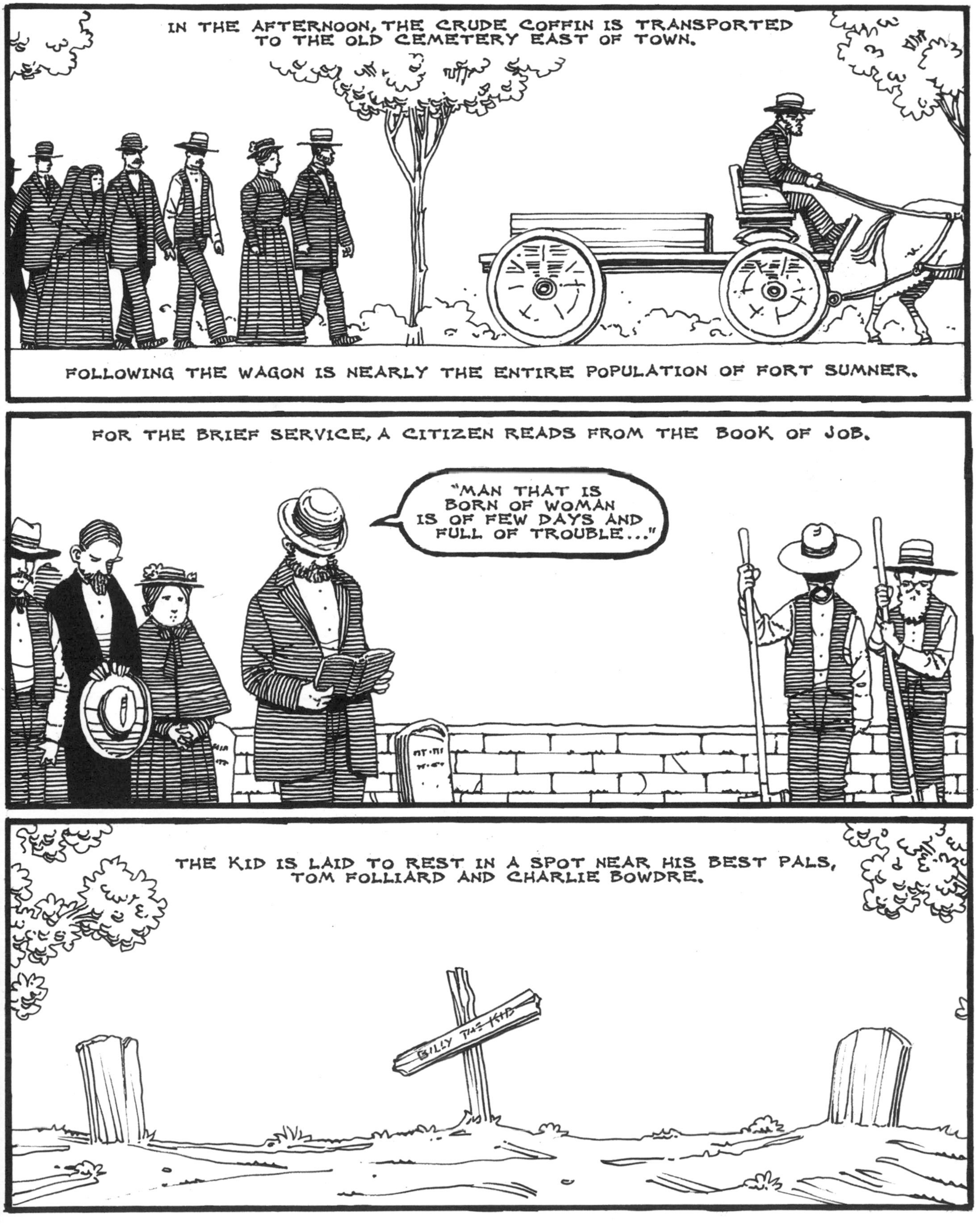

IN THE AFTERNOON, THE CRUDE COFFIN IS TRANSPORTED TO THE OLD CEMETERY EAST OF TOWN.
FOLLOWING THE WAGON IS NEARLY THE ENTIRE POPULATION OF FORT SUMNER.
FOR THE BRIEF SERVICE, A CITIZEN READS FROM THE BOOK OF JOB.
"MAN THAT IS BORN OF WOMAN IS OF FEW DAYS AND FULL OF TROUBLE..."
THE KID IS LAID TO REST IN A SPOT NEAR HIS BEST PALS, TOM FOLLIARD AND CHARLIE BOWDRE.
BILLY THE KID

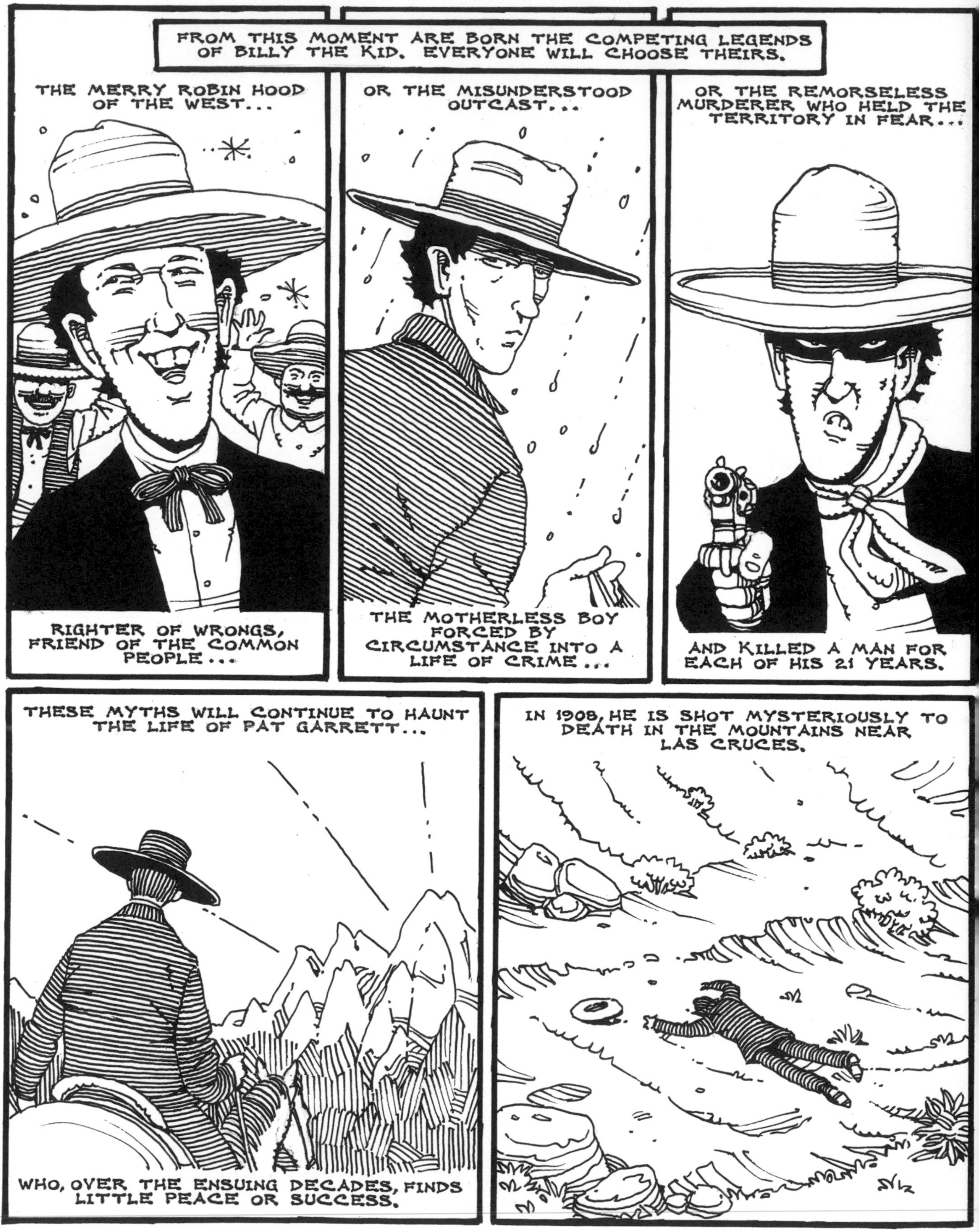
FROM THIS MOMENT ARE BORN THE COMPETING LEGENDS OF BILLY THE KID. EVERYONE WILL CHOOSE THEIRS.
THE MERRY ROBIN HOOD OF THE WEST...
RIGHTER OF WRONGS, FRIEND OF THE COMMON PEOPLE...
OR THE MISUNDERSTOOD OUTCAST...
THE MOTHERLESS BOY FORCED BY CIRCUMSTANCE INTO A LIFE OF CRIME...
OR THE REMORSELESS MURDERER WHO HELD THE TERRITORY IN FEAR...
AND KILLED A MAN FOR EACH OF HIS 21 YEARS.
THESE MYTHS WILL CONTINUE TO HAUNT THE LIFE OF PAT GARRETT...
WHO, OVER THE ENSUING DECADES, FINDS LITTLE PEACE OR SUCCESS.
IN 1908, HE IS SHOT MYSTERIOUSLY TO DEATH IN THE MOUNTAINS NEAR LAS CRUCES.

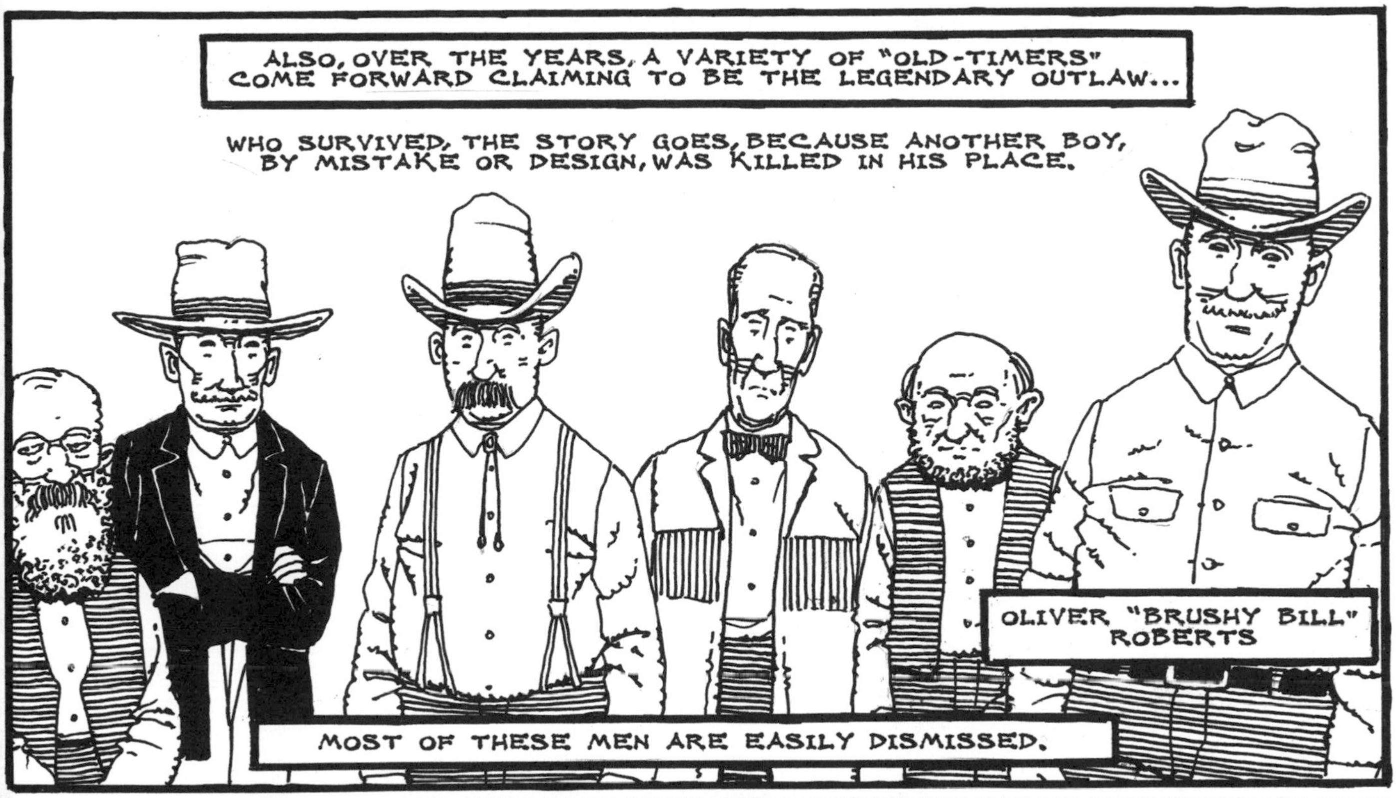
ALSO, OVER THE YEARS, A VARIETY OF "OLD-TIMERS" COME FORWARD CLAIMING TO BE THE LEGENDARY OUTLAW...
WHO SURVIVED, THE STORY GOES, BECAUSE ANOTHER BOY, BY MISTAKE OR DESIGN, WAS KILLED IN HIS PLACE.
OLIVER "BRUSHY BILL" ROBERTS
MOST OF THESE MEN ARE EASILY DISMISSED.

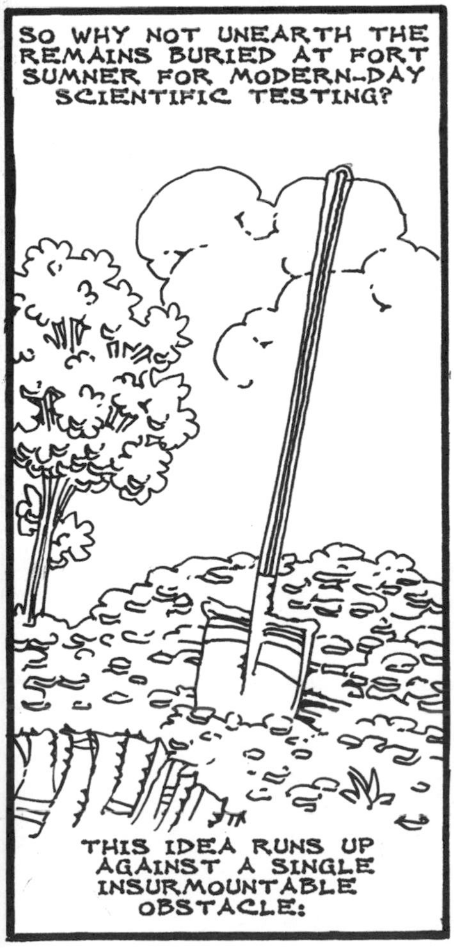
SO WHY NOT UNEARTH THE REMAINS BURIED AT FORT SUMNER FOR MODERN-DAY SCIENTIFIC TESTING?
THIS IDEA RUNS UP AGAINST A SINGLE INSURMOUNTABLE OBSTACLE:

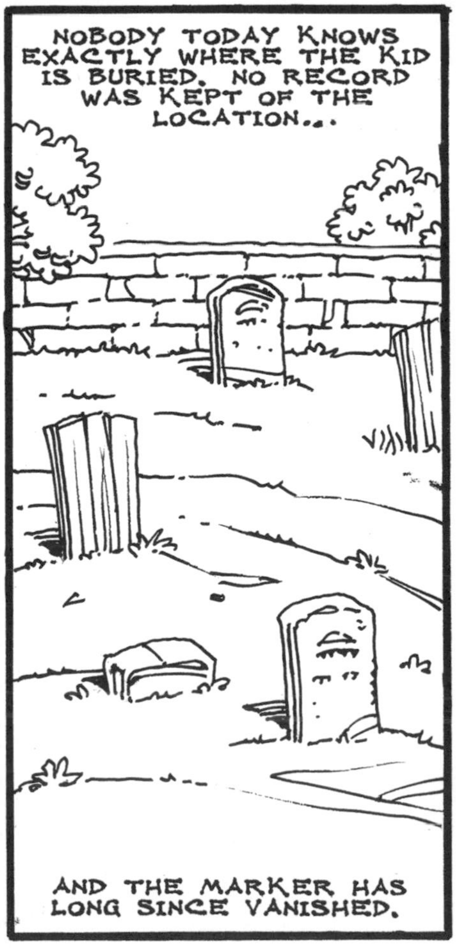
NOBODY TODAY KNOWS EXACTLY WHERE THE KID IS BURIED. NO RECORD WAS KEPT OF THE LOCATION...
AND THE MARKER HAS LONG SINCE VANISHED.

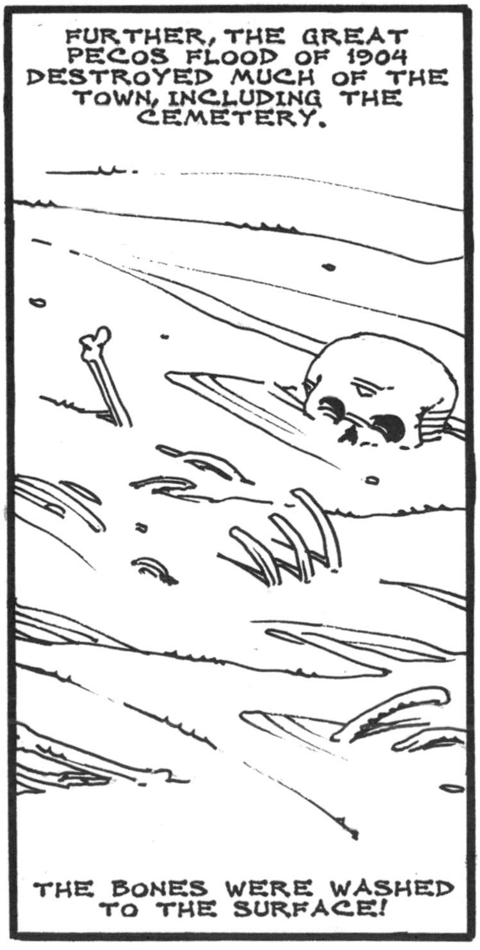
FURTHER, THE GREAT PECOS FLOOD OF 1904 DESTROYED MUCH OF THE TOWN, INCLUDING THE CEMETERY.
THE BONES WERE WASHED TO THE SURFACE!

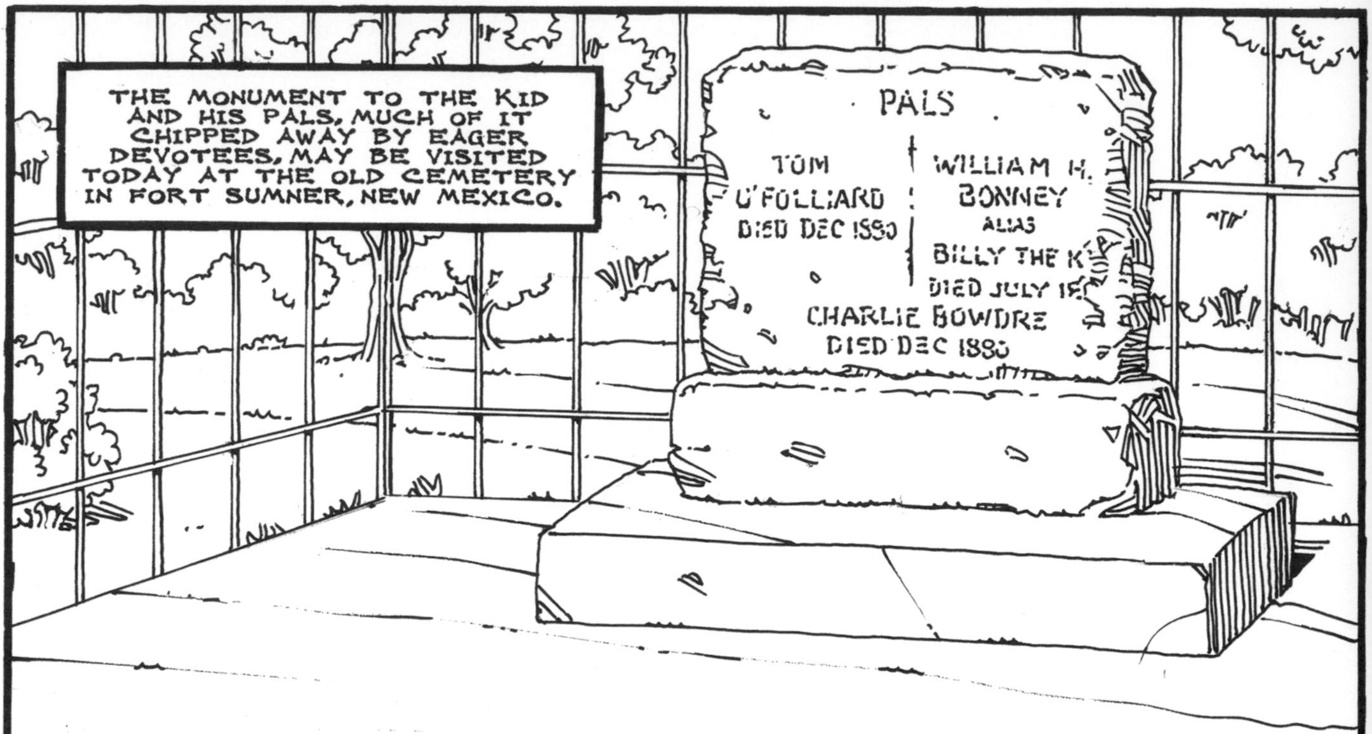
THE MONUMENT TO THE KID AND HIS PALS, MUCH OF IT CHIPPED AWAY BY EAGER DEVOTEES, MAY BE VISITED TODAY AT THE OLD CEMETERY IN FORT SUMNER, NEW MEXICO.
PALS
TOM O'FOLLIARD DIED DEC 1880
WILLIAM H. BONNEY ALIAS
CHARLIE BOWDRE

SOURCES

Bell, Bob Boze, *The Illustrated Life and Times of Billy the Kid.* (Phoenix AZ, Tri Star-Boze Publications Inc, 1996)

Cline, Donald, *Alias Billy the Kid: The Man Behind the Legend.* (Santa Fe NM, Sunstone Press, 1986)

Gardner, Mark Lee, *To Hell on a Fast Horse: The Untold Story of Billy the Kid and Pat Garrett.* (New York, William Morrow, 2010)

Nolan, Frederick, *The West of Billy the Kid.* (Norman OK, University of Oklahoma Press, 1998)

Utley, Robert M., *Billy the Kid: A Short and Violent Life.* (Lincoln NE, Bison Books, 1991)

Wallis, Michael, *Billy the Kid: The Endless Ride.* (New York, W.W. Norton & Company, 2007)

Special thanks to Gwendolyn Rogers

Rick Geary was born in 1946 in Kansas City, Missouri and grew up in Wichita, Kansas. He graduated from the University of Kansas in Lawrence, where his first cartoons were published in the University Daily Kansan.

He worked as staff artist for two weekly papers in Wichita before moving to San Diego in 1975.

He began work in comics in 1977 and was for thirteen years a contributor to the Funny Pages of National Lampoon. His comic stories have also been published in Heavy Metal, Dark Horse Comics and the DC Comics/Paradox Press Big Books. During a four-year stay in New York, his illustrations appeared regularly in The New York Times Book Review. His illustration work has also been seen in MAD, Spy, Rolling Stone, The Los Angeles Times, and American Libraries.

He has written and illustrated three children's books based on The Mask for Dark Horse and two Spider-Man children's books for Marvel. His children's comic Society of Horrors ran in Disney Adventures magazine from 1999 to 2006. He's also done comics for Gumby.

In 1989, he started the multi-volume true crime, highly acclaimed series Treasury of Murder with NBM Graphic Novels for which he is mostly known today.

In 2007, after more than thirty years in San Diego, he and his wife Deborah moved to the town of Carrizozo, New Mexico.